INTIMATE WEDDINGS

Christina Friedrichsen

NORTH LIGHT BOOKS

CINCINNATI, OHIO

www.artistsnetwork.com

Intimate Weddings. Copyright © 2004 by Christina Friedrichsen. Manufactured in the United States of America. All rights reserved. No part of this book may be reproduced in any form or by any electronic or mechanical means including information storage and retrieval systems without permission in writing from the publisher, except by a reviewer, who may quote brief passages in a review. Published by North Light Books, an imprint of F+W Publications, Inc., 4700 East Galbraith, Cincinnati, Ohio 45236. (800) 289-0963. First edition.

08 07 06 05 04   5 4 3 2 1

Library of Congress Cataloging-in-Publication Data

Friedrichsen, Christina.
Intimate Weddings / by Christina Friedrichsen.--1st. ed.
    p. cm.
Includes bibliographical references and index.
ISBN 1-55870-692-5 (pbk. : alk. paper)
1. Weddings--United States--Planning. 2. Wedding etiquette--United States.
I. Title.

HQ745.F75 2004
395.2'2--dc22

                          2004053194

Editor: Jolie Lamping Roth
Designer: Marissa Bowers
Layout Artist: Kathy Gardner
Production Coordinator: Mark Griffin
Cover Photographer: Al Parrish
Cover Photo Stylist: Jan Nickum
Author Photo: Ng's Photography

FOR DARIN,
the love of my life.

ACKNOWLEDGMENTS

A big thanks goes out to all the couples who contributed their wedding stories. They are such an important part of this book! I'm sure other couples will find the stories as interesting and helpful as I did.

Also, thank you to the photographers who generously offered wedding photos for use in this book. They make a wonderful addition to the feature stories!

I'd also like to express my gratitude to my editor, Jolie Lamping Roth, for giving me some great suggestions, as well as to my mentor, Ann Douglas, for her ideas and advice!

Finally, I'd like to thank my husband, Darin, who encouraged me, supported me, and inspired me during the entire writing process. Your patience, generosity, and kindness continue to amaze me.

CONTENTS

table of

INTRODUCTION

Your wedding. Close your eyes and envision it. What images come to mind? Do you see yourself walking down the red-carpeted aisle of a cathedral, light pouring in through stained glass windows, the scent of roses and candles filling the church? Are hundreds of guests waiting in joyful anticipation for your teary "I do"? Do you see their faces admiring you? Are many of the faces unfamiliar—your future mother-in-law's yoga instructor, co-workers you don't know well, people you probably wouldn't invite for coffee?

Or are the guests people you love who have touched you and your partner's life in special ways? Perhaps you see only seventy-five people, shining their warm smiles upon you. Maybe you see only fifty, twenty, or ten. Maybe only you and your beloved are there, exchanging vows and a sweet kiss. Everyone has her own idea of the "perfect" wedding. For some, nothing is more charming and magical than an intimate wedding.

INTIMATE IS ULTIMATE

From the moment my sweetheart, Darin, proposed to me one New Year's Eve, I knew that I didn't want a large wedding—the kind that I had been to so many times. The kind that is entirely predictable. The kind where busy brides and grooms don't have time for personal, hands-on thank-yous or one-on-one conversations with out-of-town guests.

Darin and I wanted a wedding that would suit our personalities, one that honored tradition but threw in some unique and unforgettable touches.

I soon discovered that finding information on planning an intimate wedding was not an easy task. The majority of wedding-related books were devoted to large-scale affairs, and even the Internet sites seemed to cater to couples planning big weddings. However, I connected online with dozens of other brides-to-be who, like me, thought intimate was ultimate. Many of them shared my frustration with the lack of information on this topic.

On an Internet wedding forum, a bride who was planning a wedding with fifty guests said, "I've searched high and low on the whole Internet! It seems all the planning advice is geared toward 'big weddings.'" Another bride, also at her wits end, wrote, "I believe there should be a resource out there for intimate weddings because there is really nothing out there that says having a small wedding is okay."

The number of responses to these frustrated brides showed that many couples out there lacked resources to assist them with plans for a small wedding.

Determined to change this, I set out on a mission. I spent months poring over books, magazines, and Internet sites and forums to glean as much information as I could on the topic. I interviewed wedding planners as well as couples who had tied the knot among a small group of friends and family. The more I learned, the more I realized that I could not only apply this knowledge to my own wedding but share it with others.

So after my wedding day—September 1, 2001—I began to write.

WHAT WILL YOU FIND HERE?

This book provides practical information about planning an intimate wedding. Married couples share their wedding stories. They discuss their choice to have an intimate wedding, they share advice for other couples planning a small wedding, and they let us in on anything they would have done differently. Throughout the book, I share many of my own wedding-related experiences and offer up some interesting wedding-related statistics and sidebars. Whether your small wedding will be at home or far away, whether you will marry inside a church or on a beach or in a backyard, and whether this is your first marriage or not, this book can be an invaluable planning resource.

YOUR OWN CREATION

A wedding is a creation born out of a couple's love for one another. You have every right to make your wedding uniquely yours. If you like to set yourself apart from the crowd, you will enjoy the freedom a small wedding can give you to bend the rules and create some of your own traditions. If garters, clinking glasses, and a three-tier wedding cake aren't your style, they don't have to be part of your special day.

Without a doubt, it takes a certain amount of strength to face family and friends who might be opposed to your version of an ideal wedding. The less traditional you are, the more open you will be to potential opposition from not only friends and family but also the wedding industry. Sometimes you'll need support—you'll find just that within these pages. You will read about couples who took the "aisle less traveled," who dared to listen to their hearts and have the wedding they wanted. Look in these pages for encouragement to follow your desires and create a day that fulfills all of your unique wedding dreams.

LET'S TALK MONEY

If you plan to pay for your own wedding, you will appreciate the economy of a small wedding. In this book, married couples share with you some great ideas on how to cut wedding costs for both the ceremony and the reception. An entire chapter in the book is devoted to the nitty-gritty on how to stay within a wedding budget.

At the end of most chapters, a couple's wedding is highlighted. The featured couple offers not only details on what made their day special but also a full breakdown of their wedding budget, including what they paid for flowers, photography, food, etc.

INVOLVING YOUR LOVED ONES

Have you ever been to a wedding where you didn't know a soul? A wedding with an hour-long receiving line? A wedding so large that the bride and groom couldn't spend even a few seconds conversing with you? One of the best things about a small wedding is that it enables the bride and groom to visit with each and every guest. You can make everyone feel welcome and appreciated.

If you're the type that likes to get everyone involved, you'll appreciate a small wedding.

This book shows how other couples have summoned the talents of friends and family for wedding-related tasks. Most agree that having loved ones pitch in makes the day much more memorable to everyone!

If ideas to personalize your intimate wedding are what you're looking for, you're in luck! You'll find a slew of tips on how to make both your ceremony and reception unique. Everything from writing your own vows to finding an alternative to the traditional wedding cake is discussed. You'll also find a plethora of ideas on where to have your wedding, and the chapters on theme weddings and destination weddings will spark your imagination. In the final chapter, you'll learn creative ways to preserve your wedding memories for years to come.

STORIES TO INSPIRE

Nearly three years of research and interviews led to the creation of this book. Since my mission began, I've become a wife, a mother, and now an author. Each role has brought new and exciting experiences to my life.

As the author of this book, I have enjoyed being able to connect with so many enthusiastic and creative couples. I loved learning about their unique weddings. I also derived great satisfaction from knowing that their stories, along with a ton of other great wedding-related information, would be passed along to other couples.

This truly is the book I was looking for—but couldn't find—when I was planning my intimate wedding. I sincerely believe you will find it helpful and inspiring.

Christa Friedrich

P.S. I've created a Web site to accompany this book. Please check it out at www.intimate-weddings.com. I'd love to hear from you. You can contact me at Christina@intimate-weddings.com.

CHAPTER 1

Size Matters

You've found the love of your life and you're getting married. Like most couples, you've probably talked a lot about the type of wedding you'd like to have. Maybe you've pored over Web sites and magazines, looking for ideas for planning your big day.

Whether you have a clear picture of what you want or you are still in a fog, chances are, if you are reading this book, you have one thing figured out: You don't want a big wedding.

BIGGER ISN'T ALWAYS BETTER

Perhaps you've been to enough cookie-cutter weddings—ones where the receiving line is as long as the line for a really great roller coaster—to know that a large wedding is not for you. You've decided that you want only family and good friends at your wedding. Maybe your reason for choosing a small wedding is purely financial: You simply can't imagine forking out the $20,000 that the average U.S. wedding costs. You may not have that kind of money. If you do, you'd rather spend it somewhere else, or even save it.

No matter what your reason, you've likely felt at least a bit of pressure from either the people in your life or the $72 billion wedding industry (see source: www.theknot.com) to have a white wedding with all the fixings. You don't have to feel guilty, overwhelmed, or alone if a big, fancy wedding just isn't your style. More and more couples are having the small wedding they want. Instead of enduring big, impersonal events, couples are adding intimacy and creativity to their nuptials, truly enjoying the wedding of their dreams.

With all of the advantages of an intimate wedding, it's no wonder wedding experts cite this as one of the top trends!

TEN GREAT THINGS ABOUT HAVING AN INTIMATE WEDDING

{1} **You get to celebrate one of the biggest days of your life surrounded by people who love you.** How wonderful it will be to celebrate your love for your betrothed while surrounded by dear friends and family whose joy and enthusiasm fill your heart. Of the nearly one hundred couples I interviewed for this book, almost every one said this was definitely one of the best things about having a small wedding.

{2} **You can feel more relaxed on your wedding day.** Because you'll be surrounded by friends and family, you'll feel more at home with your guests. Instead of feeling uptight, you can be yourself. If you're the type that hates the feeling of being in the spotlight, a small wedding will put you at ease. You'll feel more like part of a great get-together than the center of attention at a big, fancy shindig.

{3} **You can save money.** This is one of the most obvious advantages of having an intimate wedding, and for some it's the primary reason for paring down the guest list. An intimate wedding can save you thousands of dollars, which means your nuptials won't have to put you in debt. (For more on saving money, see chapter three.)

§4§ **You can splurge.** Perhaps you have your heart set on a high-class function with only the best of everything but know you can't afford that for hundreds of guests. By shaving down your guest list, you won't have to sacrifice your dreams of an extravagant wedding day for something less indulgent.

§5§ **You have more options when choosing a venue.** One wonderful thing about having an intimate wedding is that your choice of locations is much greater for small weddings than for big ones. Since you won't need a huge space to accommodate your guests, many doors will be open to you. According to Terry and Shannon, having a small wedding allowed them to get married in a favorite historic building in their hometown of Tecumseh, Kansas.

§6§ **You have more freedom to customize your wedding to your own tastes.** Even if you're just a tad unconventional, you'll love the freedom a small wedding will give you to break out of the traditional wedding mold and create a day that represents your uniqueness as a couple. A small wedding gives you the opportunity to get your creative juices flowing and make planning your wedding an adventure. Whether you have your wedding at a unique location or personalize your wedding with a theme, you will have many opportunities to create a wedding that reflects your personality.

§7§ **You get to spend time with your guests.** How many weddings have you attended and felt more like a spectator than a participant? How many weddings have made you feel like a stranger fulfilling a social obligation? Small weddings aren't like that. When the guest list is small, the bride and groom can spend time with each of their guests, making them feel welcome.

§8§ **You can make your guests feel at home.** Because you will be able to spend some time with your guests, they will feel more at home at your wedding. Also, when the guest list is small, guests have a better opportunity to mingle with most of the others. Chances are that many of your guests will know one another.

§9§ **You can get your guests involved.** A small wedding provides the opportunity to get your loved ones involved in your special day. Friends and family can help you with everything from decorating the reception site to reciting a poem during the ceremony. Involving friends and family helps make them part of your wedding and lightens your workload. (There's more on this later in the chapter.)

§10⅔ **You can have a wedding that people will remember.** Because your wedding won't be typical—the kind your guests have been to over and over again—your wedding will more likely be remembered. Like anything exceptional, it will stand out and leave your guests with vivid memories.

PERSONALIZING YOUR WEDDING

Your wedding day should be a manifestation of your personality. Maybe a wedding that breaks all the rules—that boldly marches to its own drumbeat—suits your style. Perhaps you fancy tradition, so a small wedding with all the rituals of a conventional wedding will make you and your fiancé feel most comfortable. Maybe the two of you are laid-back types who want a casual wedding where you and your guests can kick back and have a good time without any formalities. Conversely, maybe you want the most elegant soiree imaginable.

By having a small wedding, you and your fiancé can explore your senses of style and come up with an event that reflects the two of you.

QUESTIONS TO HELP YOU PERSONALIZE YOUR WEDDING

- Do you enjoy any hobbies? How can you incorporate them into your wedding? Perhaps you and your sweetie love the water: What about a nautical theme, or a wedding aboard a yacht? Maybe you are history buffs. Why not have your wedding at a favorite historical site and bring historical elements into your big day?

- Do you have a unique cultural background? Why not incorporate some of the culture's unique traditions into the ceremony and reception? Everything from the attire to the menu could reflect your heritage.

- Do you have a fondness for a particular season or holiday? If you both love the winter, have a winter-wonderland theme. If autumn is more your thing, bring a harvest theme into your nuptials.

- Do you enjoy the arts? You could bring artistic elements into your decor by getting married at an art gallery. The wedding reception could even include a guided tour of the gallery.

- ❦ Do you love the outdoors? Holding an outdoor wedding at one of your favorite outdoor haunts could be a soul-satisfying experience.

- ❦ Do you love to travel? You could bring your love of travel into your celebration by having a destination wedding. If you'd rather stay put for your nuptials, name tables after places you've visited, and offer foods from some of your favorite destinations.

- ❦ Are pets an important part of your life? Why not involve them in the wedding? Many a canine ring bearer has attended a bride and groom.

- ❦ Do you have a favorite restaurant? Why not have the reception there?

- ❦ Are kids a big part of your life? Consider involving them as much as possible. Kids can play roles in the ceremony or work behind the scenes to help you get ready for the big day.

- ❦ Do you enjoy writing? Why not write your own vows or a poem for your special day?

- ❦ Do you love to garden? Have the wedding in a garden, or bring fresh garden flowers into the decor. Give guests seeds, bulbs, or potted plants as favors.

A Food-and-Wine Lovers' Wedding

CARLA AND TODD, who live in Austin, Texas, brought their love of food and wine into their wedding plans. For them there was no better spot to get married than one of the country's most famous wine-producing regions—Napa, California.

Because they were each working on a Ph.D. at the time, they couldn't afford a large wedding. They didn't want to go into debt, so they decided on a guest list of nine—which kept their wedding cost down to $5,000. "We priced it out to have it in Austin, and it would have cost us around $40,000 to have our 'dream wedding.'" says Carla.

The fun began a day before the wedding, when Carla, Todd, and all of their guests toured four wineries in the region. "We had a blast! It was the first real opportunity for all of the folks to be together before the wedding; and with the wine tasting, it took the nerves away, and it ended up being a very relaxed day," says Carla. She adds that one highlight of the day was a picnic on the grounds of a winery.

The following afternoon, the couple's wedding ceremony was held at a small Catholic chapel. Keeping with the theme, Carla's maid of honor wore a wine-colored dress. The perfect choice for the reception was a restaurant called the Napa Valley Grille. "Our love of food and wine led us to this place," says Carla. A lovely private room and an affordable top-notch menu helped Carla and Todd create a special day that was truly a reflection of themselves.

CHOOSING THE PERFECT LOCATION

When Darin and I starting tossing around ideas for our wedding, we had quite a list of "maybes." Although we knew for certain that we wanted an intimate wedding, the location was a question mark.

Our first idea was Scotland. I fantasized about finding a castle in the Highlands and saying "I do" with only a minister and our parents in attendance. That possibility didn't fly: The more we thought about it, the more we wanted the rest of our family and friends to be present.

We finally decided to have our wedding ceremony at a small church and our reception at our home on the shore of Lake Erie. After all, our home was the place where we felt most comfortable and that we most enjoyed. Why not make it the backdrop for our special day? Preparing for the event ended up being more work than we could have possibly imagined, but with the help of friends and relatives we pulled it off.

When it comes to choosing a location for your intimate wedding, the possibilities are limited only by your imagination—and, of course, your pocketbook. Perhaps you consider a home—yours or a friend's or a relative's—the perfect spot for your big day. Maybe you have picked out a unique location—a vineyard, a museum, or the side of a mountain. Maybe the idea of a castle wedding is truly what makes your heart sing.

Some locations are not suitable for a small wedding. Having your ceremony in a massive church, for instance, will take away from the intimate experience and dwarf you and your guests. Likewise, having your reception in a large banquet hall, ballroom, or country club might leave you with too much empty space. Other venues, such as a favorite restaurant or inn, can offer a more intimate feel. If you get stuck for location ideas, call a few nondenominational ministers in your area. They've probably conducted weddings at all sorts of places you haven't thought of.

SIX QUESTIONS TO HELP YOU CHOOSE A LOCATION

1. Is it important for you to have your friends and relatives witness the event, or are you perfectly content to just have the two of you and maybe a couple of relatives and friends there? If the latter is true, a destination wedding can be ideal.

2. Is an outdoor wedding what you want, and are you prepared to deal with the added stress of worrying about the weather and handle the extra planning and work involved?

- Home—yours or that of a friend or relative
- Favorite vacation spot
- Bed-and-breakfast
- Hotel or inn
- Restaurant
- Skyscraper
- Museum
- Historic mansion
- Theater
- Art gallery
- Lodge or resort
- Country club
- Mountaintop
- Forest
- Park
- Amusement park or water park
- Famous landmark
- Island
- Castle
- Ranch or farm
- Beach
- Hot-air balloon

⟡3⟡ How much can you afford to spend, and is it enough to cover your ideal location?

⟡4⟡ Does the location you're considering have special meaning to you?

⟡5⟡ Is the location you're considering a practical one? Getting married on the side of a mountain might *sound* romantic, but Grandma might have trouble getting up there.

⟡6⟡ Does the site you're looking at have noise and/or alcohol restrictions?

A Laid-Back Beach Wedding

MELANIE AND ROD, from Shelby Township, Michigan, wanted to have a laid-back wedding in an exotic location without straying from the U.S. They chose a beach in St. John, U.S. Virgin Islands.

For them, it was important to invite only the people closest to them. The guest list of four included Melanie's mother, Melanie's best friend, and Rod's father and stepmother. "We decided to have a small wedding because we are not flashy people, nor do we like large crowds," says Melanie. "We wanted our wedding to be relaxing, fun, and carefree."

The morning ceremony was held on the beach under blue skies. "I just remember feeling the warmth of the sun, hearing the sound of the water and standing there with Rod, both of us perfectly at ease and being mesmerized by our surroundings," says Melanie. "The water was gorgeous shades of blue, and the backdrop provided by nature was more beautiful than any hall ... we could have rented."

The lunch reception was held at a restaurant overlooking the bay. Unlike many typical wedding receptions, there was no first dance, cake cutting, or formal speech.

Melanie and Rod agree that the best thing about their wedding, which cost $7,000, is that it was stress free. "[Planning] was very easy, and we were able to focus on the really important issue—our relationship," says Melanie. "Having the four people closest to us there made all the difference in the world."

INVOLVING FRIENDS AND FAMILY: IS IT FOR YOU?

Have a creative sister or a brother who's a computer whiz? A mother that loves to sew? What about an aunt with a special talent for flower arranging? Why not enlist their help in planning your wedding?

One of the biggest challenges Darin and I faced while preparing for our wedding was getting our house ready for the big day. Our parents and friends helped us with everything from landscaping the yard to mopping the floors. Working alongside our loved ones made the list of chores seem much less overwhelming.

For various wedding-related tasks, we called on the talents of our family and friends. My creative sister-in-law made the invitations and the place cards. My mother led the flower-arranging crew (my maid of honor, my sister-in-law, and me) in creating center-pieces, as well as the bride's and maid of honor's bouquets. Darin's talented aunt made a lovely silk ring bearer's pillow, and a friend videotaped the wedding. During the ceremony, a dear friend offered a prayer that she had written for the occasion, and my brother read one of my favorite poems. Looking back on our wedding, these moments sparkle.

Small weddings are great because you can get a lot of your guests involved. Having friends and family help you will make everyone feel a part of your big day, add a personal touch to your wedding, and leave less work for you. There's one more perk: It can save you oodles of money!

But involving friends and family is not for everyone. Some brides and grooms would rather have centerpieces from the best florist in town than have something homemade. They'd prefer embossed invitations made with the finest cardstock to invitations hand-crafted by a relative. Getting friends and family involved means to some couples less control and more stress. Some couples know what they want, but their loved ones just don't agree with their plans. In cases like these, recruiting friends and family could backfire and create long-term hard feelings.

Be grateful when family and friends offer help, but don't feel obligated to accept. Do what feels right to you.

What if, on the other hand, you want help from your family and friends but no one offers? Ask them! They might not want to butt in, and they might be afraid to approach you. You could suggest how they can be helpful to you, or you could ask them for some ideas.

If you accept help from loved ones, the best way to avoid disappointment is to be specific about what you want. If your best friend offers to wrap the candle favors, and you want them in cellophane bags tied with yellow ribbon, show her how you want them wrapped. If your brother offers to design invitations on the computer, show him examples of formats and typefaces that you prefer. Unless you are willing to just go with the flow, be clear about your ideas.

Perhaps you really want creative input from your friends and family. Ask them for suggestions, and let them show you some of their great ideas.

Gina and James, who had their seventy-guest wedding in Gina's parents' backyard, involved their entire family in the wedding. Gina's stepmother and grandmother cooked all of the food. Gina's stepsister helped get the yard ready for the ceremony; other family members helped with favors, centerpieces, and furniture setup. "It meant a lot to have our families helping us so much. We never would have gotten everything done without them. And it made the day special to know that they had put that much effort in to making the day as nice as possible for James and me," says Gina.

COMPILING THE GUEST LIST

Brides and grooms tend to be older now: The average age is twenty-five for brides and twenty-seven for grooms (see source: www.theknot.com), and many of them are well into their careers. Many a couple simply doesn't feel right asking their parents to foot the bill for their wedding. Of the 2.4 million U.S. couples that tie the knot each year, 70 percent pay for at least part of their weddings, says Richard Markel, president of the Association for Wedding Professionals International, while 30 percent pay for the whole event.

By making a significant financial contribution to their own wedding, a couple has more control over their guest list. They are not obligated to invite certain guests just for their parents' sake. Many couples choose an intimate celebration that includes only those that are near and dear to their own hearts. (If your parents are helping you foot the bill, they should have more say in whom to invite. Work with them, and do your best to compromise.)

PITCHING IN

You'll have lots of details to take care of the day after the wedding—return the tuxes, clean up, preserve your wedding bouquet, return rental chairs and tables, etc. Why not enlist the help of your family and friends?

- ☙ Decorate the venue(s)
- ☙ Drive you to the ceremony and/or reception sites
- ☙ Take photographs
- ☙ Videotape the ceremony and parts of the reception
- ☙ Read for the ceremony
- ☙ Cook the meal
- ☙ Make appetizers and/or desserts
- ☙ Bake the wedding cake
- ☙ Create centerpieces
- ☙ Wrap the favors
- ☙ Create boutonnieres and corsages
- ☙ Make the place cards
- ☙ Operate sound equipment
- ☙ Sew attendants' dresses
- ☙ Act as coordinator on your wedding day

A small guest list can mean some tough decisions. Excluding family members, friends, and co-workers is not easy—especially when there is a potential for hurt feelings. Parents might oppose the idea of a small wedding because they don't want any family members to feel left out. Uninvited friends might take offense, and people at the office might be a bit chilly knowing that they have been excluded from your big day.

It can take a great deal of inner strength to face opposition from those around you, and the best way to handle it is with honesty. Tell anyone who might feel hurt because they aren't invited that you and your fiancé have chosen to have a small wedding with only a few close friends and family members. Tell them that number limitations meant that many people were left off the guest list. You might even explain to them why you have chosen an intimate wedding, so they will better understand your position. Some people still won't get it. Remember, you can't please everyone. Being true to yourselves is what really matters.

Amanda and Jose had been to plenty of large weddings (Amanda's cousin had 720 people at her wedding!) and didn't want more than fifty people on their guest list. This meant they had to be selective when making their list. "We didn't even invite the best man's girlfriend of three years because we didn't know her. Everyone who was at the wedding had some kind of impact on our lives at one point or another," says Amanda.

Some couples choose to have a postwedding party for family and friends who aren't invited to the wedding. This gives people a chance to celebrate in an informal way, and it can ease hurt feelings.

Kristen and Stephen had a postwedding party after their restaurant reception. "We had planned an 'after party' later in the night, . . . a very casual affair [to] which we were able to invite all our friends and co-workers that we could not invite to the wedding," explains Kristen.

QUESTIONS TO ASK WHEN MAKING THE GUEST LIST

- ❀ Are we inviting this person simply because we feel obligated to? If she invited you to her wedding, you might feel obliged to return the favor.

- ❀ Have we seen this person within the last year?

- ❀ Does this person have a significant other? If not, is it necessary for him to bring a guest?

- ❀ Do we want to invite children?

- ❀ Is it necessary to invite our co-workers?

INVITING CHILDREN

For some couples, inviting children is a must. For others, keeping the wedding to adults only helps to keep the guest list small. If you decide not to invite some children, be fair. Inviting your best friend's kids and not your brother's kids might make for some hard feelings.

CREATING INVITATIONS

The style of your invitations can let your guests know what type of wedding you are having, so why not get creative? You may have a fondness for traditional invitations—ivory cardstock with vellum overlays and formal lettering and wording—but you have countless other creative options. If you plan a small wedding, you have the opportunity to custom make your invitations or to purchase truly unique ones.

One option for brides and grooms who want something truly unique is to send a message in a bottle. At The Message in a Bottle Shop (www.bottlemeamessage.com), from DreamWeaver Studios, you just input your message; they will print your invitations, put them in a bottle, and send them either to you or directly to all of your guests. If you are crafty and would like to make your own message in a bottle, go to UltimateWedding.com (www.ultimatewedding.com) for instructions. From the home page, click on Resources. Under Article Categories, select Invitations and Announcements. A list of article names will follow. Select "The Creative Invitation—Message in a Bottle" by Denise S. Webster.

Couples who want to make their own invitations will appreciate the many interesting types of paper available—including handmade paper. For an outdoor garden wedding, for instance, you could use a paper made with botanicals. Hand-pressed flowers can be added for an extra touch. For the lettering, you could hire a calligrapher or create the lettering yourself on the computer. In fact, with all the desktop publishing software available, it's possible to make attractive invitations on the computer. All you need, aside from some good, quality paper, is a little creativity and a bit of computer skill. No matter what style of stationery suits you, get creative, and have some fun with your invitations! (For more on creating invitations, see the Resources section at the back of this book.)

FOR THOSE WHO AREN'T INVITED

It's courteous to send to family and friends who aren't invited an announcement to let them know that the wedding took place. Wedding announcements are usually worded similar to an invitation and get sent as soon as possible after the wedding. Be aware that some people feel such announcements are purely solicitations for wedding gifts, so consider adding a "no wedding presents" message.

MAP IT OUT

Try to get your invitations out four to six weeks before the big day—and don't forget to include a map.

A Summer Wedding at Home

~

CHRISTINA & DARIN

AMHERSTBURG, ONTARIO, CANADA

THE MEETING:	Darin and I met on an IRC (Internet Relay Chat) in 1997. After the first "hello," we quickly became great friends. We traveled to Scandinavia together before becoming a couple in the summer of 1998.
THE PROPOSAL:	Darin and I had just spent the last evening of the twentieth century celebrating at my parents' house. When we got home, we plunked down on the couch, and much to my surprise, Darin handed me a shiny silver package. Inside it was a jack-in-the-box that I had recently been eyeing at a local jewelry store. When I opened up the box, Jack popped out with a sparkling engagement ring pinned to his little hand— and then Darin proposed.
CEREMONY:	St. Andrew's Presbyterian Church in Amherstburg, Ontario, Canada
RECEPTION:	Outdoors under a tent at the couple's home
NUMBER OF GUESTS:	50
COST:	$8,000 ($10,400 CAD); paid for by the bride and groom, with some help from both sets of parents
PLANNING DURATION:	6 months

Darin and I had been to enough large-scale weddings to rule out that option. We didn't want a wedding with a mile-long receiving line. We didn't want a wedding that made us feel as though we were onstage. We wanted to be ourselves.

Having a small wedding also allowed us to splurge on the things that really mattered to us: great food, great music, and ambience. Keeping the guest list small wasn't very difficult. Darin is an only child, and he didn't have a lot of family members to invite. Because I work at home, I didn't have to worry about inviting co-workers—I don't have any, unless you count the two dogs and three cats that like to hang out in my office and wreak havoc on my workspace! Neither of us felt it was necessary to invite Darin's co-workers.

We didn't start planning our wedding until six months before the big day, but we knew early on that we wanted to have the reception at our home. Darin and I had bought a house on a lake two years before and thought it would be an ideal setting for our nuptials.

PLANNING

Even though our wedding was small, it took a great deal of planning. Darin and I had a strong idea of what we wanted, and it took plenty of work to make it happen. For me the planning process was trying at times, but mostly it was a fun challenge. I liked most that it involved plenty of creativity.

I turned to Internet forums for ideas and support. No books on small weddings were available, so I spent many hours searching for information online. Some particularly helpful sites were Frugalbride.com (www.frugalbride.com), Talk About Weddings (www.talkaboutweddings.com), WeddingChannel.com (www.weddingchannel.com), and The Destination and Specialty Wedding Web Ring (www-personal.umich.edu/~kzaruba/wedding.html).

Unlike some brides you'll read about, I didn't purchase anything for the wedding online. I probably could have saved quite a bit of money by doing some shopping in cyberspace.

AN INDOOR CEREMONY

Darin and I decided three months before the wedding that we wanted to have a church wedding instead of an outdoor ceremony at our home. Planning for the home reception was enough work without having to accommodate the ceremony as well. After talking about it at length, we agreed that we'd be happy saying our vows inside a small church.

We chose St. Andrew's Presbyterian for several reasons. First, we liked the minister. During our initial visit to the church, the minister was very warm and welcoming. Second, the church, which has a rich history in the community, is beautiful and small enough to suit our wedding plans.

The ceremony was short, simple, and lovely. To add meaning, my brother read "Love Poem" by Kathleen Raine, and a dear friend of mine read a prayer she had written for the occasion. When it was over, a bagpiper piped us out of the church with "Scotland the Brave."

THE RECEPTION: CREATING AMBIENCE

Darin and I wanted to incorporate the garden theme into the reception. We spent the entire summer landscaping the yard and filling the flower beds with impatiens of all colors. We placed the reception tent right next to the flower beds, which by that time of year were positively exploding with color.

A local florist decorated the inside perimeter of the tent with tulle and twinkle lights. Tulle was also draped along the center poles. Nearly two dozen votive candles were placed inside the tent to help create an enchanting atmosphere after dark. Garden bouquets with mauve, yellow, and white flowers—including alstroemerias, roses, button mums, and gerbera daisies—served as the centerpieces. They looked beautiful on the white linen tablecloths on each of the six round tables.

My mother, along with my maid of honor and various family members (including me), stayed up past midnight the night before the wedding creating the centerpieces as well as the bridal bouquet and the maid of honor's bouquet. I'll never forget the sight of the laundry room—our makeshift workshop—covered in discarded leaves and flower petals. It was quite a spectacle! Not only did we create some priceless memories, but we saved quite a bit of money by purchasing the flowers wholesale at a local greenhouse and making the flower arrangements ourselves.

Lovely pressed-flower name cards that my sister-in-law had created also brought the garden theme into the tent. Each name card was unique and made a nice keepsake for each one of our guests.

Instead of numbering the tables inside the tent, we named the tables after famous works of art. We made color copies of the artworks and displayed them at each table.

Soapmaking is one of my hobbies, so we gave handcrafted bars of soap in fragrances of lavender, rose, peppermint, vanilla, and bay rum as favors. The favors were packaged in small cellophane confectionary bags wrapped with ribbon.

A BIG SURPRISE

Although we first thought about having a cocktail reception, we decided it would be more fun to stretch out the evening with dinner and music. After a delicious, catered, sit-down meal, guests were entertained with a few short speeches and a live Celtic trio that played some of our favorite Irish music.

But the highlight of the reception happened before all of that. Without telling anyone, including me, my husband had arranged to have a Scottish pipe band pipe us into our reception. I was speechless! The band marched along our driveway and played some of the most incredible Scottish music I had ever heard. Each of our guests was completely "wowed" by the experience, and I was the happiest new bride in the universe!

LOOKING BACK

I loved having a small wedding. I enjoyed spending time with the guests, and I loved seeing them have a good time. After dinner, I remember looking at one of the tables where a group of guests was absolutely roaring with laughter. It felt great knowing that people were having fun.

Throughout the day I kept in mind some advice I had read on an online wedding forum: Stay in the moment. I was so glad to be able to be truly "present" during our special day instead of passing through it in a busy blur. I was able to take the time to soak it all in and to enjoy every minute. Not only did this awareness make for a wonderful day; it also provided me with some vivid memories that I will cherish for a lifetime.

BRIDE TO BRIDE

- Get your sweetie involved in the planning. It will make it easier—and more fun.
- Don't think that a small wedding won't require many hours of planning— especially if you want to have the wedding at your home.
- When family and friends offer to help, take them up on it! Make sure you let them know what you need—and what you don't need. We were so grateful to our families for helping. It made less work for us and made our wedding even more special because so many people we cared about played a role.

Christina

Christina and Darin's Wedding Budget

Reception venue, food, and beverages *(including cake and service)*	$3,850
Attire	$950
Flowers	$750
Photography	$1,070
Stationery *(sister-in-law made the invitations)*	$0
Gifts	$250
Wedding rings	$550
Ceremony	$330
Transportation and parking	$150
Miscellaneous expenses *(favors)*	$100
Total	**$8,000**

The Planning Stages

If anything was irritating while Darin and I were planning our wedding,

it was wedding timelines—the ones in the back of many wedding books.

I'd read them and suddenly be flushed with panic. "Oh no, we're two

months behind on ordering my dress. And look at this—we're four months

behind on choosing a caterer!" But then I'd come to my senses and remember

that these timelines are generally geared for big, traditional weddings.

Besides they're only guidelines. Not everyone plans their wedding a year in

advance. I know of one couple who planned their eighty-person wedding

(which included horses!) in only three days.

So, this chapter provides "to do" lists instead of a rigid timeline. These

lists are only suggestions. Use what pertains to you, and disregard the rest.

TO DO BEFORE THE WEDDING

The lists in this section give you a general idea of what needs to be done before you say "I do." Rearrange, add, and delete items to fit your priorities.

GETTING ORGANIZED

Wedding planning generates a lot of paperwork. A good way to organize the paperwork is by topic. Use a separate folder for each topic, such as photography, caterer, officiant, etc. Keep the folders in a binder or other file storage container for easy access.

☑ IN THE BEGINNING . . .

☐ Announce your engagement to friends and family. They might throw you a party or at least treat you to a meal.

☐ Decide what type of wedding you want to have. Do you want a church wedding or a bed-and-breakfast wedding? Will your wedding be indoors or outdoors? Will it be formal or casual? How many people will you invite? (See chapters one, six, and seven.)

☐ Look at your finances and decide how much you want to spend on your wedding. If loved ones will contribute, find out how much they plan to give. (See chapter three.)

☐ Choose venues for the ceremony and reception or one venue where you can hold both. If you choose an outdoor venue, contact tent rental companies. (See chapters six and seven.)

☐ Choose an officiant. (See chapter four.)

☐ Pick a date. This may hinge on what dates are available for your chosen site(s).

☐ If you will hire a caterer, start looking around and sampling some food. (See chapter five.)

☐ Meet with photographers and videographers and ask to see representative samples of their work. (See chapters four and five.)

☐ Choose a florist. If you plan to do your own flower arrangements, check around for places that sell flowers wholesale.

☐ If you will have live entertainment at your celebration, start listening to some musicians. The ones that are good and not overpriced will probably book up fast. If you will have a deejay, start searching for a good one. (See chapters five and seven.)

☐ Keeping in mind the style of your wedding, decide on attire. If you need a formal wedding dress, start shopping at bridal stores or online [eBay (www.ebay.com) is one of many sites where you can find a wedding dress]. If you are planning a more casual event, check out area department stores. Think about the temperatures if you will have an outdoor wedding. Whatever the venue, choose something that not only suits the occasion but is comfortable. (See chapters six, seven, and ten.)

☐ Choose attendants, and ask them to be in your wedding.

☑ **A LITTLE LATER ON . . .**

☐ Make your guest list. If you will invite out-of-town guests or have a destination wedding, let guests know your wedding date well in advance. If appropriate, consider sending save-the-date cards. (See chapters one and nine.)

☐ Meet with your officiant to discuss the format of the ceremony.

☐ Choose a photographer and/or videographer, and decide on a package.

☐ Hire a caterer, and discuss the menu.

☐ Make a final decision on entertainment. Book the band or deejay.

☐ Choose floral arrangements. Meet with a florist, if necessary.

☐ Order or make the invitations and programs. If you will make either, start now. Also decide on place cards. If you will make the place cards, start creating them. (See chapters one, four, and eight.)

☐ Make arrangements for tuxedos or other formalwear.

☐ Register for wedding gifts. Choose a traditional registry if you want to stock your household, or select another option. You can open a honeymoon registry, where guests help you pay for your honeymoon. You can register for stocks (check out www.greenwish.com). If you want someone else to benefit from your wedding, go to www.justgive.org/weddings/index.jsp and arrange for guests to donate to charity instead of buying gifts for you. (See chapter three.)

☐ Book your honeymoon travel and lodging.

☐ Shop for wedding rings.

☐ Select a type of wedding cake. If the caterer will not supply the cake, find a baker.

☐ Book transportation if you want a limo or other rented vehicle for your wedding day.

Exceeding the budget is one of the top concerns of brides [source: Hallmark Press Room (http://pressroom.hallmark.com)]. For helpful tips on staying within your budget, see chapter three.

□ Choose a hairstylist and makeup artist (if you want one), and book these appointments.

□ Choose wedding shoes and accessories, and buy or borrow them, if necessary.

☑ **CLOSER TO YOUR WEDDING DAY . . .**

□ Send invitations. The general rule for timing is six to eight weeks before the big day.

□ Have final meeting with officiant.

□ Choose the location of your rehearsal dinner, and make any necessary reservations.

□ Purchase your wedding license. Each state is different when it comes to the waiting period involved in attaining a marriage license, the amount of time that the license is valid, and whether or not a blood test is required. To find out about the laws in your state check out www.weddingdetails.com/questions/license.cfm.

□ Go for a trial run on your hair and makeup.

□ Attend gown fittings and formalwear fittings.

Wedding Day Itinerary

Consider making a list of wedding day events and giving it to your wedding party, as well as other friends and family who will take part in your wedding, before the big day. The list will keep everyone abreast of the activities and leave less room for potential mishaps.

☑ **EVEN CLOSER TO YOUR WEDDING DAY . . .**

□ Pick up the wedding dress. Make sure you try on your dress early enough so that alterations can be made if necessary. Allow time for the dress to be steamed.

□ Create your seating plan.

□ Purchase or make gifts for each other and for the attendants.

□ Call to confirm each vendor. This should be done one to two weeks before your wedding day.

□ Send thank-you notes for gifts you receive prior to the wedding.

□ Pick up formalwear.

□ Write checks for vendors if you know final amounts in advance.

□ Pack for your wedding night and honeymoon.

TO DO AFTER YOUR WEDDING DAY

The tasks don't end after the "I dos." There are still a few items that need to be accomplished. Thankfully, you can kick back and enjoy your honeymoon before tackling these final details.

☐ Send wedding announcements soon after your wedding, preferably as soon as you return from your honeymoon.

☐ Send thank-you notes within one to two months after returning from your honeymoon.

☐ Process name and address changes if necessary.

☐ Put together your wedding scrapbook. (See chapter eleven.)

☐ Create an online photo album for friends and family to view. An online album will give your loved ones instant access to your wedding photos. (See chapter eleven.)

BUTTON CHECK

When the groom and his attendants pick up the tuxedos, they should check all the buttons to make sure they are on nice and snug. (My sister-in-law had to fix one of Darin's jacket buttons at the last minute.)

CHAPTER 3

A Budget That Works

Before you book the venue, buy the dress, and pick out the flowers, there's something you and your sweetheart must do: figure out how much you can afford to spend on your wedding.

Perhaps you dread this more than any other aspect of planning your wedding. Perhaps this is enough to make you want to hide beneath the covers and scream, "Make it go away!" Or maybe you're one of the lucky ones who derive sweet satisfaction from meeting financial challenges head-on. Whether you fit into one of these categories or fall somewhere in between, your wedding budget will play a key role in your wedding plans.

TO SAVE OR TO SPLURGE?

Perhaps your budget is the sole reason you want a small wedding. Maybe you looked good and hard at your finances and reasoned that a large wedding would put you and yours in serious debt. Maybe you decided that you'd rather slim down your budget and save the extra cash for a down payment on a house. Or perhaps the two of you agreed that you'd rather funnel money into your investments than blow thousands on a one-day event.

Although a small guest list can give you the opportunity to save thousands of dollars, smaller doesn't always mean cheaper. Some brides and grooms decide to have fewer guests and splurge on the wedding, pulling out all the stops. In this chapter, you'll read about one such couple as well as other couples who had weddings on minimal budgets.

HOW MUCH CAN YOU AFFORD?

Maybe you're the type that "oohs" and "aahs" over pictures in bridal magazines. And you've opted for a small affair, but you'd still love to have a "Martha Stewart" wedding— with everything from clusters of fresh roses on every table to an array of petit fours from the finest bakery in town. Maybe you really want to go all out on your wedding. Now for the hard part: Can you afford it, or will it put you and your honey in debt for years to come?

If you charge thousands of dollars in wedding expenses on your credit cards, you could end up paying a lot more for your wedding than you ever imagined. To illustrate: Say you charge $5,000 of your wedding-related items on a credit card with an annual interest rate of 18 percent. If you make just the minimum payments of $100 per month, it would take you more than seven years to pay off the debt, and you'd pay not only the $5,000 but also approximately $4,300 in interest!

The best way to stay within a budget you can afford is to start planning early and begin saving for your wedding months ahead. Opening up a wedding savings account can be a good idea. Putting 10 percent of each paycheck into the account can make for a sizable chunk of cash after several months.

Planning ahead will also give you time to comparison shop and find bargains. Clearance sales can save you a bundle!

When it comes to your wedding budget, both of you should get involved and keep

DO YOU HATE FINANCIAL PLANNING?

If you're clueless about financial planning, check out www.Ihatefinancialplanning.com. It has plenty of tips for people who think financial planning is as fun as cleaning out the dust bunnies behind the fridge.

did $_{YOU}$ know ?

According to The Knot (www.theknot.com), the average U.S. wedding budget is $20,000. If you were to invest $20,000 and earn interest at an annual rate of 6 percent, you'd have $36,388 in ten years; $66,204 in twenty years; and $120,452 after thirty years.

close tabs on your wedding expenses. Just because you're having a small wedding doesn't mean those expenses can't add up quickly!

To keep track of your budget, you can use a spreadsheet program like Microsoft Excel or WordPerfect Quattro Pro. List the items and services you purchase, input costs next to each item (don't forget sales tax!), and keep a running tally.

WHERE YOUR MONEY WILL GO

Even though your wedding will be small, you can still expect to spend most of your budget on your reception. Unless you will simply serve appetizers or have friends and family make the meal, food and beverages will account for a good portion of your wedding expenses.

Other significant expenses include entertainment, attire, flowers, and photography; and the ceremony is generally one of the least-expensive pieces. Below is a chart showing a typical budget breakdown.

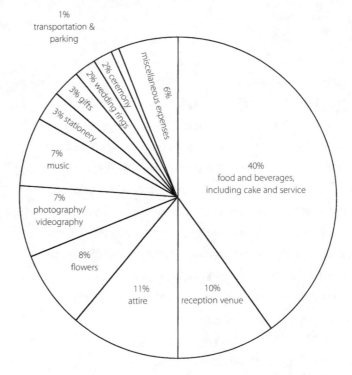

Source: The Knot's Complete Guide to Weddings in the Real World.

SETTING PRIORITIES

According to some wedding experts, the two things that your guests will remember the most from your wedding are the food and the entertainment. I think this especially rings true for large weddings.

Of the many big weddings I have attended, I can't say I remember what each bride and groom wore. I don't remember how the churches were decorated or what the centerpieces looked like. I don't remember a thing about what was said during the speeches or who caught the bridal bouquet. But I do remember the meals and the music.

When you invite only close friends and family, something as simple as a barbecue with hot dogs and hamburgers for your reception can be just as unforgettable as a five-course, sit-down meal at a high-end bistro. The intimacy that you and your guests feel will make your wedding especially memorable, and every couple has their own idea of what is important.

Some couples might be happy with hamburgers and use the money they save on food to hire a top-notch, ten-piece band. Some brides might not give a hoot about flowers but want to spend a small fortune on the wedding dress. The key is to work together as a couple, be very clear about your priorities, and realize that spending money on some things might mean you'll have to sacrifice other wedding details.

did *YOU* **know**?

The average household income for newly married couples is $51,591. [source: The Knot (www.theknot.com)]

For Shannon and Robert, who had eight people at their wedding, certain wedding items were essential. "For me it was custom-designed invitations," says Shannon, who adds that they spent 25 percent of the wedding budget on handmade invitations.

Plated meals were also a must and accounted for 50 percent of the budget. "One of the things we enjoy doing with our friends is going out for dinner, so we decided that having an amazing meal was the second most important thing, after the ceremony."

For Darin and me, meals and music were at the top of the list. In fact, we spent nearly half of our wedding budget on these two items alone. Another important element was wedding photography. I have a keen interest in photography and couldn't imagine not having a professional capture our big day.

When setting budgets, some couples decide they can save money by hiring an amateur photographer or having a friend or family member shoot the wedding. The result can be mediocre photos and a less-than-satisfied couple—but this does not always happen.

An amateur photographer, along with family and friends, took Linda and Mickey's wedding photographs. "I am really impressed by some of the photos taken by my maid of honor and my family," says Linda.

did *YOU* know?

In the U.S, the average amount spent on photography and videography for a wedding is $1,260. *[source: USA TODAY.com (www.usatoday.com)]*

Hiring a professional does not automatically mean you will be happy with the photographs. Several couples I interviewed were dissatisfied with their professionally taken photos.

Dana and Christopher, for instance, were sorely disappointed with their photographer. "We had problems with him from the outset, culminating in a disaster at the wedding," says Dana. "We ended up with lousy pictures, very few of the pictures we'd requested, and nothing worth enlarging. Thank goodness many of our friends brought cameras and took great candids."

Remember: Your wedding lasts a day, but your photographs will last generations. If that is important to you, make sure you do plenty of research before hiring a photographer—and listen to your gut. If you find a photographer you like, make sure he provides you with references so that you can talk to other couples about his work. It also helps if you like him. You don't want to spend one of the most special days of your life (and believe me, you'll spend plenty of time with the photographer) with someone you can't stand! (For more on photography, see chapters four and five.)

QUALITY OVER QUANTITY

Many couples choose to have a small wedding because they want to go all out. They want to dazzle their guests with delicious food, great entertainment, and gorgeous surroundings. A large guest list wouldn't allow them to have these things. These couples would rather have an intimate wedding and splurge on their guests than have a large wedding where their dreams and expectations have to be compromised.

WEDDINGS BETWEEN $15,000 AND $20,000

Heather and Anthony, for instance, spent $15,000 on their wedding attended by sixty-seven guests. "By having a small wedding, we were able to spend money on the things that we felt were important," says Heather. "If we [had] had a large wedding, we couldn't have had it at the Emerson (a historic inn in Rockport, Massachusetts), where the food is absolutely fantastic. We wanted people to have a fabulous meal."

For Cari and Jeremy, who had sixty-five people at their $17,000 wedding held at a lodge in Colorado, great food was also important. "A small wedding enabled us to have the kind of event we really wanted—with fabulous food and drink and lots of details we wouldn't have been able to afford with a large number of guests," says Cari.

These couples have no regrets about choosing quality over quantity.

An Elegant Inn Wedding

REBECCA AND ANDREW wanted only the finest for their Pennsylvania wedding. They knew from the beginning that they wanted a small wedding with sophistication and warmth. "Having a small wedding meant we could have the best of everything without going into debt," says Rebecca. She and Andrew spent nearly $20,000 on their wedding, which had fifty-nine guests.

The New Jersey couple got married at a Lutheran church that had special meaning to Rebecca. "I was born into this church, my grandparents attended this church, my parents attended this church, and it's beautiful inside. [It has] great stained glass windows."

For the reception site, the couple chose an inn that had a fitting atmosphere and quality food. "Our cocktail hour was in a three-room farmhouse with a fireplace blazing. The main reception room had wooden banisters and huge picture windows. It was more of a warm and comfortable setting than a cold, impersonal one, like so many larger weddings I have been to," says Rebecca.

Along with food and atmosphere, music was a priority for the couple. A violinist and an organist played during the ceremony. During the reception's cocktail hour, a four-piece string quartet provided music, and after dinner, a ten-piece band got everyone dancing.

Another priority for the couple was flowers. For the bouquets, as well as the flowers for the church, Rebecca chose gardenias to honor her deceased grandmother. (Gardenias were her grandmother's favorite flower.) The budget for their small wedding allowed the couple to splurge on attendants' gifts and a luxurious eleven-day honeymoon in Italy.

Rebecca and Andrew's Wedding Budget

Reception venue, food, and beverages (including cake and service)	$12,000
Attire	$1,000
Flowers	$1,000
Photography/videography	$1,000
Stationery	$200
Gifts	$2,500
Wedding rings	$150
Ceremony	$250

Transportation and parking	$500
Favors	$480
Total	**$19,080**

WEDDINGS BETWEEN $10,000 AND $15,000

Perhaps you don't want to go overboard on your wedding, but you still want a few splurges here and there. Maybe a wedding between $10,000 and $15,000 fits your budget. Whether you choose to say your nuptials in your hometown or away, it shouldn't be too difficult to plan an enjoyable small wedding that fits this budget.

Las Vegas Nuptials

DANA AND CHRISTOPHER, who live in Peoria, Arizona, have friends all over the country. So they decided to have their springtime wedding in a city that they knew everyone would enjoy—Las Vegas. "This was a once-in-a-lifetime opportunity to have them all in one place at one time," says Dana.

The couple paid for the wedding themselves and had a budget of $10,000. Keeping costs down was a priority, so they opted for a guest list of thirty-five. Luckily, both Dana and Christopher have small families, so making the guest list wasn't difficult.

Having a small wedding allowed the couple to indulge their guests in a few extras, including a rehearsal dinner attended by all the guests, as well as a postwedding brunch. The couple opted for a short, simple ceremony at the Little Chapel of the Flowers for sentimental reasons: It's the chapel where Dana's parents and grandparents tied the knot. The dinner reception was held on an outdoor patio at Victoria's in Las Vegas. The couple chose this location for the outdoor option—and because the price included food, beverages, deejay, table linens, centerpieces, and cake. After the party at Victoria's, the couple and their guests were whisked off in rented buses to the couple's hotel, where the festivities continued at an on-site bar.

To stay within their budget, Dana and Christopher had to make a few sacrifices here and there. Instead of buying a high-end designer gown, Dana chose a less expensive one. Dana also had her makeup done by her sister-in-law rather than a professional, and she skipped the "luxurious spa day" she had hoped to enjoy before the ceremony. Although the couple wanted to pay for the guests' hotel rooms (with a welcome basket in each room), they found that it would not fit their budget. The couple also saved money by:

- Making their own invitations. Each one cost $1 before postage.
- Using the chapel's flowers and pew decorations instead of buying their own.
- Sticking with the reception decorations that were included in the wedding package at Victoria's. All Dana added were a few rose petals on each table.
- Having the dress altered somewhere other than a bridal shop. This was much less expensive.

- Purchasing a white gold ring for Christopher, instead of a platinum one.
- Buying no new accessory jewelry except an inexpensive bracelet for the wedding. Dana wore her mother's necklace and her own diamond earrings.
- Buying wedding shoes for $12 at a discount shoe store.

Dana and Christopher's Wedding Budget

Reception venue, music, food, and beverages *(including cake and service)*	$3,000
Attire	$715
Flowers	$300
Photography/videography	$1,300
Stationery *(includes invitations, response cards, thank you cards, etc.)*	$225
Gifts	$325
Wedding rings	$600
Ceremony	$500
Transportation and parking	$800
Miscellaneous expenses *(chair rental, archway and other decorations, favors, bride and groom's lodging, rehearsal dinner, and preliminary visits to location)*	$2,325
Total	**$10,090**

WEDDINGS UNDER $5,000

Whether your wedding is just the two of you and a beach or sixty of your loved ones in your parents' backyard, you can have a charming wedding without diving headfirst into deep debt. Obviously, a smaller guest list gives you more opportunity to save.

If you're on a really tight budget, an elopement or a destination wedding with just a couple of family members might be the answer. (See chapter nine for more on destination weddings.) If, however, you want to stay in town for your nuptials with a few more people, you still have countless ways to save money.

Many couples have thrown a knockout wedding for under $5,000. You can do that too, but it will take a bit of creativity—and some legwork.

A Wedding Potluck in the Park

RACHEL AND DAVID, both in their twenties when they married, played by their own rules when it came to their wedding. As a result, they saved thousands of dollars. "We literally threw convention to the wind," says Rachel.

With a budget under $2,000, the bride and groom had to be resourceful when planning their special day. They decided to have a potluck picnic for about seventy-five guests at a local park in Richland, Washington; the cost to rent a portion of the park was less than $100 for the day.

After a short morning ceremony outdoors in the park, guests enjoyed a luncheon reception there. "We couldn't afford anything fancy, and knowing how much our families enjoy getting together for picnics and barbecues, we knew they wouldn't at all mind pitching in," says Rachel.

And pitch in they did. Rachel's mom brought all the sandwich fixings, while other guests brought drinks, salads, munchies, and desserts. David's aunt even made the wedding cake.

Rachel and David were able to keep their costs low by many other means:

- Instead of buying a wedding dress, Rachel borrowed her cousin's wedding dress.
- Rachel made her bridal bouquet, the bridesmaids' bouquets, and the boutonnieres out of silk flowers.
- Rachel's two bridesmaids and two flower girls wore sundresses that Rachel's mom and aunt and David's mom sewed.
- The flower girls carried recycled baskets that the couple spray painted white and filled with rose petals from a friend's garden.
- Instead of hiring a deejay, Rachel and David borrowed sound equipment from a friend and played CDs.

Rachel and David have no regrets about deciding to have a wedding that cost them less than $2,000. "I'm really glad we didn't splurge. To me it wasn't how much money was spent but the overall atmosphere [that was important]. It was a beautiful, warm, sunny day … and we were surrounded by family and friends. That's all we cared about," says Rachel.

Rachel and David's Wedding Budget

Reception venue, music, food, and beverages *(including cake and service)*	$175
Attire	$200
Flowers	$100
Photography/videography	$150
Stationery	$50
Gifts	$0
Wedding rings	$1,100
Ceremony	$0

Transportation and parking	$0
Miscellaneous expenses	$200
(chair rental, archway and other decorations)	
Total	**$1,975**

FIFTY WAYS TO SAVE ON YOUR EXPENSES

From the moment you begin your journey into the world of wedding planning you have opportunities to save money. Here are some ideas to get you started:

STATIONERY:

§1§ Make your own invitations, or have a friend or family member make them for you. Check out WeddingClipart.com (www.weddingclipart.com) for clip art and templates.

§2§ Instead of including response cards with the invitations, save the postage and include an e-mail address and/or phone number for responses.

§3§ Buy your invitations online. There is more selection online, which means it is easier to find invitations to fit your budget. In many cases you buy direct from online sources, so you cut out the middleman and the markup. Some Web sites to check are www.theamericanwedding.com, www.regencyinvitations.com, and www.paperstyle.com.

ATTIRE:

§4§ If a fancy designer gown is not a must, consider renting a wedding dress or buying one secondhand. There are often wedding dresses—some never worn—advertised in the classified section of newspapers.

§5§ Buy a dress online. Sites such as eBay (www.ebay.com) can offer significant savings on wedding dresses, both secondhand and brand new. Sites such as The Bridal World (www.thebridalworld.com) offer warehouse prices on new wedding dresses.

§6§ Consider buying a discontinued dress from a bridal store.

§7§ If you are planning a casual wedding, check out the dresses at area department stores.

§8§ Do the guys really need tuxedos? Maybe suits would look fine.

§9§ A bride who's into crafts can make her own veil and headpiece. Materials are plentiful at craft and fabric stores, and instructions are available on the Internet and in books.

§10§ Buy inexpensive shoes. If the bride's gown is long, no one will see the shoes anyway. Ballet slippers can be purchased from a dance studio for a reasonable price.

§11§ Borrow a friend's crinoline.

§12§ Buy bridesmaids' dresses from a department store.

§13§ Do your own hair and makeup.

FLOWERS:

§14§ Use flowers that are in season, and use plenty of greenery in the bouquets.

§15§ Pick out some pretty garden bouquets from the grocery store, a flower wholesaler, or a greenhouse instead of going to a florist.

§16§ Bring the floral arrangements from the ceremony to the reception site instead of buying separate ones.

CENTERPIECES:

§17§ Use floating candles instead of floral centerpieces.

§18§ Place a single flower in a bud vase or float a single flower in a bowl of water instead of using a full arrangement.

§19§ Use potted plants instead of cut flowers.

DECOR:

§20§ Lots of balloons in colors that complement your wedding theme are a great alternative to more-expensive decorations.

§21§ Buy some tulle and twinkle lights, and decorate the venue yourself.

FAVORS:

§22§ Dollar stores can be great sources for favors. They usually have candles galore, and they have fun stuff for your child guests.

TRANSPORTATION:

§23§ Instead of renting a limo, rent a fun car, such as a Volkswagen Beetle or a convertible Ford Thunderbird, and have a friend play chauffeur.

§24§ Use your car or that of a friend or family member to transport you from the ceremony to the reception.

REHEARSAL DINNER:

§25§ Is an elegant rehearsal dinner necessary? If not, consider a more casual dinner. You could go out for Chinese food or order a pizza or even have a backyard barbecue.

VENUES:

§26§ Have your wedding during the off-season (November 1 to April 30).

§27§ Get married on a Friday night or on Sunday.

§28§ Have a Christmastime wedding. Chances are the venue will already be decorated.

§29§ Hold the ceremony and reception at the same location. You're likely to have a lower total rental fee—and you'll save money on transportation and decorations.

§30§ Choose a venue that needs little adornment, such as a garden or decorated facility.

FOOD:

§31§ Serve appetizers on a buffet instead of having servers circulate them.

§32§ Ask friends or family to make the appetizers and desserts.

§33§ Consider having a cocktail reception instead of a sit-down meal.

§34§ Have a brunch or lunch reception, or provide a buffet instead of a plated meal.

§35§ Have a potluck reception.

§36§ Use the wedding cake as the dessert. (Everyone will be stuffed anyway!)

§37§ Borrow seldom-used items such as the punch bowl and cake knife instead of purchasing them.

WEDDING CAKE:

§38§ Instead of a wedding cake, order a fancy cake from a bakery. (Who doesn't love cheesecake!)

§39§ Decorate the top of your cake with fresh flowers or fruit instead of a cake topper.

ALCOHOL:

§40§ Have an open bar, but limit the selection of beverages. Instead of offering hard liquor and mixed drinks, allow the guests to choose from wine, beer, wine coolers, and soft drinks.

§41§ Choose a venue where you can supply your own alcohol.

§42§ Make your own wine and beer at a do-it-yourself place.

§43§ Offer poured service rather than leaving the wine bottles on the tables.

§44§ Don't bother with champagne for the toast. Guests can toast with whatever they are drinking.

MUSIC:

§45§ Hire one musician to play at both the ceremony and the reception.

DOUGHNUTS ANYONE?

Want for your wedding a fun and inexpensive dessert that will be sure to get everyone talking? What about Krispy Kreme doughnuts? More and more couples are buying dozens of doughnuts to serve to their guests at the reception. Some couples have a cake decorator stack the doughnuts, or fancy them up a bit. Other couples purchase two- or four-packs as gifts for their guests.

{46} Instead of hiring a deejay, create your own CD compilations and play them throughout the reception.

PHOTOGRAPHY/VIDEOGRAPHY:

{47} Have a professional shoot the standard shots, and opt for the basic package. For all the other photos, provide guests with disposable cameras or ask friends and family to bring their cameras.

{48} Call a local university or college to find out about any talented student photographers that shoot weddings.

{49} Call your local newspaper to find out if any of the photojournalists do weddings.

{50} Instead of hiring a professional, have a friend videotape the service.

USE THE INTERNET TO SAVE MONEY

More and more brides- and grooms-to-be are turning to the Internet to help with their wedding plans. The Internet is a great source for providing general planning information and cutting wedding costs. Couples find they can save hundreds—even thousands—by surfing. Everything from invitations to wedding dresses to photographers can be found online.

Judy and Justin, from New York City, made great use of the Internet when planning their wedding. They searched cyberspace for everything from a reception site to a minister to a place to buy seed packets.

Judy, who says she did the majority of the wedding planning, also found a limousine company and even a wedding photographer online. "We found our wedding photographer after posting an ad on an online photography forum," says Judy. "He is a professional photographer who wanted to break into the wedding business. He offered to do our wedding for a ridiculously low fee, and we snatched him up after seeing his [work] online."

Judy also made good use of eBay, where she ordered bubbles, ribbons, and seed packets. If you are interested in online shopping for your wedding, see the Resources section at the back of this book for Web site information on everything from attire to favors.

FEWER GUESTS, FEWER GIFTS

Some couples I interviewed mentioned that the one drawback of having a small wedding was that they received fewer gifts. It's true. You will receive fewer gifts, which means you'll probably receive less cash to help pay for your wedding expenses.

However, you can make the gifts you do receive count toward one of your wedding expenses—your honeymoon. Traditional gift registries are great for couples who need household items; but if you already have a toaster, a cupboard full of dishes, and a closet full of linens, a honeymoon registry is ideal. Couples register with a travel agent or an online honeymoon registry service (such as www.thebigday.com, www.giftpile.com, www.afterIdo.com, or www.honeyluna.com) and create a list of honeymoon gifts they would like to receive. A wish list could include airfare, resort accommodations, and even romantic gifts such as a candlelit dinner, a luxurious massage, or an afternoon of horseback riding. Guests simply choose from the list the gift they would like to purchase for the couple, just as they would use a traditional registry.

If your honeymoon is already covered and you have all the household items you need, consider setting up a charity registry. The I Do Foundation (www.idofoundation.org), for instance, allows couples to share the generosity of their guests directly with the couple's chosen charitable cause. Guests simply make online donations in lieu of purchasing wedding gifts.

did *YOU* ?
know !

People spend $19 billion per year on wedding gift registries. *[source: The Knot (www.theknot.com)]*

WEDDING INSURANCE: COVERING YOUR ASSETS

It's the morning of your wedding. You bolt out of bed and peek out the window to see if the weatherperson's prediction of thunderstorms came true. Sure enough, the sky is black, and the wind is snapping branches left and right. You turn on the television, and much to your horror a tornado warning has been issued.

When it comes to weddings, Mother Nature doesn't always cooperate—and she's not the only one who can wreak havoc on your wedding plans. What if you or your fiancé suddenly contracts a gastrointestinal virus on your wedding day? What if your caterer decides to close up shop a day before your wedding and skip town with your deposit? What if someone steals the wedding gown you left in the backseat of your car?

With all the things that can possibly go wrong, some couples decide to play it safe and buy wedding insurance. A U.S. company called WedSafe (www.wedsafe.com) is one company that offers an insurance policy covering various wedding-related mishaps. (Fireman's Fund also offers wedding insurance. See Resources, page 184.) If weather, illness, or a death in the family causes wedding cancellation or postponement, the company will reimburse you for the costs. If your wedding gifts are stolen, if the wedding dress or the groom's tux is damaged, or if your limo driver or your photographer doesn't show up, you're covered. A liability and property damage policy can also be purchased. This policy protects you from liability related to certain types of accidents that might occur during the wedding or reception and result in bodily injury or property damage. Be warned: One thing the policy doesn't cover is cold feet.

A Beautiful Wedding on a Budget

~

SHANNON & ERIK

ROSEVILLE, MICHIGAN

THE MEETING:	Shannon and Erik met online through an Internet friend-finder company. Shannon, who lived in Washington state at the time, vowed she wouldn't get involved in a long-distance relationship—but that changed when she and Erik began corresponding. After three months of e-mails and phone conversations, Shannon flew to Michigan to meet Erik in person for the first time. "It was love at first sight," she says. Eighteen days later, she packed her bags and moved to Michigan.
THE PROPOSAL:	Erik chose Valentine's Day to propose to Shannon. Although the proposal wasn't a big surprise for Shannon—she knew that Erik had purchased her ring—she was elated nonetheless when an excited Erik got down on his knees and popped the question.
CEREMONY:	Healing Water Tabernacle Church, Roseville, Michigan
RECEPTION:	Athena Hall, Roseville, Michigan
NUMBER OF GUESTS:	38
COST:	$3,740; paid for mostly by the bride and groom
PLANNING DURATION:	2 months

Despite having thirty-eight guests and a sit-down meal, Shannon and Erik, both in their twenties when they married, were able to keep the budget for their October wedding under $4,000.

Shannon and Erik chose to have a short traditional ceremony at a small church in Michigan. "[The church's] atmosphere was light and friendly." The reception was held at a family-owned hall.

Because the couple married on Sweetest Day, they decorated the hall with pink heart balloons and silk roses. They also used navy and white balloons.

GOING FRUGAL

To purchase the balloons—and other wedding-related merchandise—Shannon and Erik made great use of discount stores and eBay. "EBay is a godsend for small weddings. There is no way we could have had a wedding without it," says Shannon. "We paid for this wedding ourselves and could not afford the prices that wedding merchandisers charge elsewhere." All of the items that the couple purchased on eBay were brand new. Here are some items they bought online:

- Shannon's wedding dress: $200 ("It was going for $1,000 in the store," says Shannon.)

- Cathedral-length veil: $40

- Mini veil (worn at the reception): $10

- Five tuxedos (for the groom, three groomsmen, and Erik's dad), including jackets, pants, vests, and ties: $40 each

- Five shirts: $20 total

- Silk wedding flowers, including the bridal bouquet, three bridesmaids' bouquets, an arrangement for the bouquet toss, and ten lapel flowers: $80

- Wedding ring set: $40 ("They are brand new matching ten-carat gold rings with etching, …I got a ton of compliments on these," says Shannon.)

- Wedding invitations: $20 ("We bought a wedding invite kit and printed them and stuffed them ourselves.")

- Church decorations, including a wedding arch, vines, tulle, pew bows, an aisle runner, bubbles for the grand exit, and a wedding chest to hold the rings: $75

- Reception decorations, including a silk centerpiece for the head table, eight disposable wedding cameras for guests, refreshment trays, party napkins, champagne glasses, balloons, and three-foot (ninety-one centimeters) tall wedding bears (bride and groom) to stand at the entrance: $150

The couple didn't use only online sources to cut costs. Shannon and Erik also shopped around town for the best prices and bought from discount stores. Here are some other ways they cut costs:

- For the hall reception, Shannon and Erik were able to bring their own liquor— much of it purchased at Sam's Club and Costco at bulk rates. "This saved us $4 a person," says Shannon.

- Instead of renting champagne glasses, the couple purchased some from a discount store. The glasses cost $10 per dozen.
- Instead of having the hall provide dessert, the couple made some dessert items themselves and purchased others from a bakery. A friend who is a professional wedding cake decorator made the wedding cake for $150.
- For the centerpieces, the couple purchased glass bowls from a dollar store and filled them with marbles and floating candles. The couple purchased helium tanks from Costco and decorated the venue with balloons.
- Instead of hiring a professional photographer, Shannon and Erik had a friend shoot the wedding with a digital camera. The cost was $100—with no additional developing fee.
- On their wedding day, the couple used Erik's sports car instead of renting a limo.

ATTIRE

Although Shannon had tried on several dresses at bridal shops, she bought her dress online. "The person I purchased from had a high enough selling history that I was comfortable buying from her. I also figured that if I didn't like the dress it was early enough before my wedding that I could sell it back to someone on eBay and find a new dress," Shannon says. But that didn't happen. "I absolutely loved it!" she says.

To make sure the dress would fit, Shannon researched how wedding dresses are sized, then she simply bought a dress in her size range. "The dress fit perfectly except in the chest area, so I purchased a corset off eBay to use instead of having the dress sized."

When choosing dresses for her three bridesmaids, Shannon selected a color that she knew would be practical. "We went with easy-to-find wedding colors so that there would not be any special pricing or dyeing charges," she says. The bridesmaids' dresses cost only $30 a piece at a department store. The dresses were not all the same, but they were all navy blue. Instead of spending a fortune on shoes, Shannon and her bridesmaids bought shoes from a discount shoe store during a "buy one, get one for half price" sale. Shannon gave the bridesmaids the dresses, the shoes, and a trip to the hair salon as attendants' gifts.

Erik gave the three groomsmen and his father tuxedos, which included jackets, pants, vests, and ties. Erik bought the tuxedos, even one for himself, on eBay. "They were Christian Dior," says Shannon. "They came from a tuxedo shop, but they were [the prior] year's models." Along with the tuxedos, Erik gave the groomsmen shirts, also purchased online.

SAVING MONEY

Shannon and Erik say they feel great about throwing their wedding for under $4,000. They have some sage advice for other couples who want to keep their wedding costs low: "Make it, bake it … or bring it yourself," says Shannon.

On eBay purchases:

· Know the rating of the seller. Repeat sellers have received feedback from their buyers.

· Shop around. Look at many companies and auction sites online to get the best price.

· Don't get caught up in the auction frenzy. Determine your maximum bid and stick to it, or you may end up paying more than an item is worth.

Shannon

Shannon and Erik's Wedding Budget

Reception venue, music, food, and beverages *(including cake and service)*	$1,950
Attire	$1,100
Flowers	$90
Photography/videography	$100
Stationery	$20
Gifts *(included in "Attire")*	$0
Wedding rings	$40
Ceremony	$150
Transportation and parking	$0
Miscellaneous expenses *(decorations for ceremony and reception)*	$290
Total	**$3,740**

CHAPTER 4

Creating an Intimate Ceremony

If I failed to recognize anything about the wedding ceremony until my wedding day, it's how quickly the ceremony goes. All that planning, all that anticipation, all that excitement—and in twenty minutes it's over.

That doesn't mean the time, energy, and creativity that go into planning it are wasted. Twenty minutes may not seem like a big chunk of time, but it's enough time to create a heap of wonderful memories. You can bet that mental snapshots of those few special moments will stay with you for a lifetime.

THE AISLE LESS TRAVELED

Darin and I had a traditional Presbyterian ceremony, but if I had to do it over again I'd be less formal and more creative. Although we personalized the ceremony by having loved ones recite selected poems and prayers, we could have added other special touches to make the ceremony even more suited to our personalities. Whether you want your ceremony to vary only slightly from tradition or to be completely customized to your personalities, you'll find that having a small wedding gives you the freedom to create a wedding that is true to both of you.

Many of the couples I interviewed wrote their own vows and incorporated unique rituals into their ceremonies. The guests formed a circle around one couple during the ceremony. Another couple hugged all of their guests after the vows instead of heading straight down the aisle.

That's the beauty of a small ceremony: You can be creative *and* bring intimacy into every moment. You and your mate will feel that, and your guests will enjoy it, too.

Jane and Mike, who got married at an Episcopalian church, included communion during their wedding ceremony. "The guests surprised us. Almost everyone came up for communion or a blessing," says Jane. "We wouldn't have had time to do this at a larger wedding." The couple felt the communion helped them connect with their guests in a unique way.

Linda and Robert added a special touch to their estate wedding in Florida by having a dove release. "[We] released two white doves from a beautiful heart-shaped box to symbolize our union," says Linda.

Other couples added personal touches to their weddings by twisting the rules a bit. Instead of having just her father walk her down the aisle, Jan had both her mom and dad do the honor. "The pastor kept trying to nix it, but I stood my ground," says Jan.

Elisabeth, on the other hand, had her brother walk her down the aisle. Initially, Elisabeth could not decide whether or not to have her father or her stepfather walk her down the aisle, so Elisabeth chose her mother to do the honors. When her mother died three months before the wedding, Elisabeth decided she'd go it alone. "I wasn't going to have anyone walk me down the aisle. It didn't feel right unless she was there," Elisabeth says. However, five minutes before the ceremony, Elisabeth decided to ask her brother to accompany her to the altar.

Love Doves

Interested in having a dove release at your wedding? Get the scoop at www.white-dove-releases.com.

47

CIVIL OR RELIGIOUS?

Early on you'll need to decide whether your ceremony will be civil or religious. If neither of you has church affiliations or wants any religious elements in your wedding, you can opt for a civil ceremony conducted by a legal official such as a justice of the peace, a judge, or a notary public, or by a nondenominational cleric. If you attend a house of worship, you'll probably opt for a religious ceremony.

Here are some other reasons you might choose a civil ceremony:

- ☙ Your officiant isn't flexible about the structure of the ceremony. He doesn't like your nontraditional ideas and won't stray from the norm.

- ☙ You want a simple, quick, and uncomplicated wedding.

- ☙ It's not your first marriage, and your religious institution doesn't approve.

- ☙ You two come from different religious backgrounds and can't decide which one to marry under.

A civil ceremony doesn't mean you can't have a wedding with attendants and other wedding ceremony traditions. It does means you can get as creative as you want with all the ceremonial nitty-gritty—including the location.

Not all couples who choose a religious ceremony are worshipers. Some haven't stepped inside a house of worship for years. Darin and I did not regularly attend church, but we both felt it was important to have a service that included some spirituality.

Religious ceremonies—often held inside a church, synagogue, or mosque—can take place in a variety of locations, depending on the flexibility of the officiant. Many non-denominational clerics will marry couples just about anywhere. (For more on church weddings, see chapter six.)

FINDING AN OFFICIANT

If you want a religious ceremony and aren't members of a house of worship, the hunt for an officiant can be a challenge. Some couples choose to marry where their parents or grandparents married, which makes things easier. Other couples might choose a church merely for its aesthetic appeal and then take the officiant who comes with the church.

Although aesthetics definitely played a role for Darin and me, we also wanted an officiant who made us feel comfortable. We visited several churches before deciding on a local

Presbyterian church. (Neither of us are Presbyterians.) The officiant was friendly, and the church was the perfect size for an intimate ceremony—and it was beautiful.

If you're looking for an officiant, visit local churches, or simply search the yellow pages or the Internet. Start your search as soon as possible to ensure an officiant's availability. (For a list of questions to ask a potential officiant, see page 92.)

To make your wedding even more personalized, have a friend or loved one act as your wedding officiant. Christine's oldest and dearest friend became licensed as a marriage commissioner in order to officiate at Christine's wedding. "We worked on the ceremony together and wrote the entire thing from scratch. She did a fabulous job," says Christine.

A friend of Christina and James performed their ceremony. He was ordained online. "We wrote our own vows. . . . It was very personal," says Christina.

Becoming certified as an officiant can be quite simple. Wedding Ministers Online (www.uncas.net/wedding) offers certification online for a nominal fee. The only other requirement is filling out a form at the Web site. The Universal Life Church, a non-denominational church, offers free ordination—online or via snail mail (see Resources, page 184)—to anyone who requests it.

CHOOSING ATTENDANTS

Having a whole crew of bridesmaids doting over me on my big day definitely would not have suited me. I wanted simplicity; one maid of honor and one flower girl was just perfect for me. My husband felt the same way and chose only a best man and a ring bearer as his attendants.

Some brides and grooms, however, love the idea of having a huge bridal party. For these couples, having lots of loved ones by their side makes the day more fun and special.

Some couples choose a team of attendants simply because they feel pressured to do so. Perhaps they've stood up in friends' weddings and feel obligated to return the favor. Maybe they feel as though a slew of attendants is a wedding requirement.

After speaking to numerous couples, I'm glad to say that the rules about attendants are changing—especially for intimate weddings. Some brides and grooms choose to have no attendants, and others ask their mothers, fathers, or children to stand with them. Gender roles have changed, too. Men choose women as honor attendants and vice versa. A friend of mine, for instance, served as her brother's "best woman."

You should feel free to ask the most special person in your life aside from your sweetie to serve as your honor attendant even if that person is of the opposite sex. If you consider

If a child is old
enough to appreci-
ate money, put a quarter
or two where the child
is to stand. If the child stands
nicely on the coin(s) for
the ceremony, the child
keeps the coin(s).

your mother to be your best friend, have her take on the role. You can even go it alone. Do whatever feels right.

INVOLVING FAMILY AND FRIENDS

Because of the personal nature of an intimate ceremony, involving loved ones seems natural. Whether you have five guests or fifty, you have many options for including your friends and family.

Having a loved one perform a reading during the ceremony is a wonderful way to get someone close to you involved. My oldest brother read a favorite poem during our ceremony, and a dear friend said a prayer that she had written especially for us.

Those who suffer stage fright might serve as ushers or work behind the scenes before the ceremony. If there are children—your own or someone else's—in your life, you can find several ways to get them involved. Flower girls, ring bearers, and junior bridesmaids can all add special charm to your wedding—and the children will have unforgettable experiences. Keep in mind that not all children enjoy the spotlight. Some children may prefer to distribute wedding programs, light candles, or hand out bubbles for blowing after the ceremony.

If you decide to include children in your ceremony, keep in mind that kids can be unpredictable. If you're the type that can't handle little surprises, you might want to leave the participation to the adults.

LET'S TALK TUNES

Can you imagine a wedding ceremony without music? Could a bride walk down the aisle without a tune to carry her to the altar? What kind of recessional would have no joyous song of celebration?

I can't imagine a wedding ceremony without music. Perhaps if vows were exchanged on a beach or in a forest, where the sounds of the ocean or singing birds or windblown trees would sweetly fill the silence and remove the need for music. Otherwise, music is an integral component of a ceremony. It sets the mood and stirs emotions—and it's a great way to personalize a ceremony.

No instrument on Earth hits me smack dab in the heart like bagpipes do. They give me a shiver along my spine like one that can come during the national anthem or a great, poignant movie ending. For me there was no question about having a bagpiper at our wedding. Sure we also had an organist, but the bagpipes were the main musical event.

When it came to choosing the songs the bagpiper would play, we decided to go with some familiar Scottish tunes. After all, who doesn't love "Scotland the Brave"? We had the organist play some traditional wedding music, such as Bach's "Ode to Joy." We stuck with traditional music for no other reason than because we felt moved by the melodies.

For Kerry and John, a spirited rendition of "Amazing Grace" was the musical highlight of their ceremony. Everyone in the church joined in singing the classic hymn just before

CEREMONY MUSIC

TRADITIONAL SELECTIONS

Prelude:
- "Water Music" by Handel
- "Air on the G-String" by Bach
- "Violin Concerto in A" by Haydn

Processional:
- "Canon in D" by Pachelbel
- "Wedding March" by Mozart
- "Trumpet Voluntary" ("Prince of Denmark's March") by Clarke

Interlude:
- "Ave Maria" by Schubert
- "Arioso" by Bach
- "Let the Bright Seraphim" by Handel

Recessional:
- "Ode to Joy" by Beethoven
- "Wedding March" by Mendelssohn
- "Trumpet Tune in C" by Purcell

CONTEMPORARY SELECTIONS

Prelude:
- "A Whiter Shade of Pale" by Annie Lennox
- "More Than This" by Roxy Music
- "No Ordinary Love" by Sade

Processional:
- "Caribbean Blue" by Enya
- "Only Time" by Enya

Interlude:
- "By Your Side" by Sade
- "Unforgettable" by Natalie Cole
- "Nocturne" by Secret Garden

Recessional:
- "Love Song" by Ronan Hardiman
- "Isma Vova" by Elise Velle
- "One by One" by Enya

(Note: If you will have a church ceremony and want nontraditional music, your officiant might want to okay your selections.)

the couple was pronounced husband and wife. "People really sang it out," says Kerry.

Not all couples, however, feel compelled to stick with tradition when they select music. Gina and James used the music of Enya for their ceremony. "I walked down the aisle to 'Only Time' and we walked out after the ceremony to 'One by One," says Gina.

Linda and Evan had the theme song from *Rocky* for their recessional. "[It's] Evan's favorite movie—he loves it," says Linda. "Our guests kind of chuckled; it was really cute. Since it was a small gathering [about fifty guests], they all knew about Evan's love of the movie and knew it was special."

Besides your selection of music, your choice of musicians will help to personalize your ceremony. Some couples prefer live music—any combination of instrumentalists and vocalists. If you have a talented musician in the family or a friend who sings or plays an instrument, you might ask her to perform during the ceremony. This can add an even more personal touch.

Other couples prefer to use recorded music. Perhaps they don't want to pay for hiring a live musician, or maybe they love a song as performed by the original artist.

Sit down with your sweetheart early on and discuss your preferences. If you insist on traditional wedding music but your honey wants some contemporary tunes on CD, why not compromise and have both? Do what suits you as a couple, and don't be afraid to be daring.

A Church Ceremony With a Personal Touch

MELODY AND DOMINIC decided that an intimate wedding with fifty-two guests would be perfect for celebrating their love and devotion to one another.

As a professionally trained vocalist, Melody had attended her share of large weddings—and she knew that she definitely didn't want one. "I have seen way too many weddings become three-ring circuses," she says.

The couple, who paid for their wedding themselves (it cost less than $5,000), decided to have their ceremony at a historical church in Lansing, Michigan. They were very familiar with the church: Dominic was the church's business administrator at the time.

The 11 A.M. ceremony started with Melody performing a portion of the prelude music, singing Bach's "Jesu, Joy of Man's Desiring" and Mozart's "Alleluia." "The scene was gorgeous. . . . The sun streamed brilliantly through the stained glass windows of the church," says Melody.

Following the prelude, Melody watched her attendants walk down the aisle. Then, with her mother holding her hand, Melody walked to the altar to the sounds of Beethoven's "Hallelujah Chorus."

Melody made a point to take in every moment of the ceremony. "I remember everything. I made certain that I would. From the look of absolute stage fright on my husband's face to his [near-tears brother and best man]," she says.

"I remembered being awfully happy that I could see everyone and look everyone in the face as I walked down the aisle with my mother."

But the highlight of the ceremony wasn't walking down the aisle. It wasn't the vows either. The best part came at the end. Just after the ceremony, the couple's wedding coordinator hustled them downstairs into a room where they could have a few seconds of privacy to enjoy their brand-new status as husband and wife. Thinking that they were alone, Melody expressed her excitement to her new husband. "I just remember being hysterical and pressing my fore-head into his, saying, 'We did it! We actually did it!'" Little did she know that the moment would be captured forever on film. "Our photographer must have snapped the picture at that very moment before the coordinator slammed the door in the poor man's face," says Melody. "Seeing that picture [brings] back that breathless endorphin rush of actually pulling it off, of completing a life-changing event that neither of us had ever planned on going anywhere near."

WRITING YOUR OWN VOWS

Although some clergy members might discourage you from writing your own vows, many are open to this creative option. Several of the couples I interviewed wrote their own vows and were very pleased with the outcome.

For Keely and Xan, the exchange of their self-written vows was the most powerful part of their intimate wedding. "They were the most meaningful words I have ever uttered. I could hear myself say them, and wow, it was amazing," says Keely. "In those few minutes that we swore to share our lives, my life took on new meaning."

Lynette and Charles also wrote their own vows. This not only added intimacy to the ceremony; it made it more meaningful and emotional. "We did not share them with one another beforehand. He read his first, and he was on the verge of tears. . . . Then, when it was time for me to read mine, I had to take what seemed like an eternity to compose myself because I was about to start bawling," says Lynette. "I am one [who] rarely shows emotion like that, but I was so moved I almost could not contain myself."

If you are considering writing your own vows, keep these things in mind:

- **It can be time consuming.** If you're a perfectionist and feel as though you need to nail down precisely how you feel about your partner, the writing process could take a while. The solution: Keep it simple.

- **It can be difficult, especially if you don't enjoy writing.** Love is a hard thing to express on paper—even for those who make careers of putting words together. If you have difficulty expressing yourself in words, writing your own vows could be a horribly laborious process. The solution: Start by simply writing down how you feel about your partner and your upcoming marriage and what it all means to you. You could do this like a love letter to your beloved. From there, convert your thoughts to vows. For an even simpler route, find in books or on the Internet some samples of vows that you like and revise them to suit you.

⊛ **It can rattle your nerves.** Do you get stage fright? Does the thought of speaking in front of a group of people give you the jitters? If you write your own vows, you might feel extra nervous about delivering them, especially since they will be so emotionally charged. The solution: Keep it short. Also, if you don't want the added pressure of memorizing your vows, use note cards.

If you need ideas to get you started, you can look at various Web sites that offer sample vows, such as Brilliant Wedding Pages (www.brilliantweddingpages.com/couples/sample_vows.asp) and UltimateWedding.com (www.ultimatewedding.com/vows).

Ceremony From the Heart

SHANNON AND ROBERT, who hail from Bedford, Texas, had a difficult time finding a church to get married in, so they opted for a hotel wedding. "The colors and style of everything from the stained concrete floors to the art deco couches and chairs in the lobby to the wonderful art hanging on the walls emanated the look and feel we were attempting to achieve," says Shannon.

The couple originally planned to have thirty guests, but after Shannon got laid off from work, they had to scale back the guest list to eight. "We both take our marriage very seriously, and we wanted the people that knew us best and loved us most to be there when we committed our lives to one another," says Shannon.

Because both of them felt that the ceremony was the most important part of the wedding, they put a great deal of thought into planning it. Shannon spent several months visualizing every element of the wedding ceremony. " I envisioned lots of candlelight. That is why we had our wedding the weekend we did. It was the first weekend after the fall time change [back to standard time]. I wanted it [to be] dark for our 6 P.M. affair," says Shannon.

By using a variety of candles as their only light source other than a few white twinkle lights and the violinist's small light, the couple transformed a hotel meeting room into an elegant, glowing ceremonial space. Shannon says the look was "almost medieval."

Even though they did not want a "religious" ceremony, they did want an ordained minister to marry them. Many of the ministers they contacted would not marry them because the couple lived together or because the couple did not belong to the congregation. Through the Internet, Shannon and Robert found a nondenominational minister/theology professor to perform the role.

Shannon had only one attendant: Her sister acted as her maid of honor. Robert had two of his best friends as attendants.

Shannon and Robert wanted their wedding to be highly personal, so they wrote the entire ceremony themselves, pulling from different ceremonies they found online. Their wedding vows captured the essence of how they felt about their commitment to one another:

Robert: I ROBERT, TAKE YOU SHANNON, TO BE NO OTHER THAN YOURSELF. LOVING WHAT I KNOW OF YOU, TRUSTING WHAT I DO NOT YET KNOW. WITH RESPECT FOR YOUR INTEGRITY, AND FAITH IN YOUR LOVE FOR ME, THROUGH ALL OUR YEARS AND IN ALL THAT LIFE MAY BRING US, THROUGH THE BEST AND THE WORST, I WILL LOVE YOU FAITHFULLY.

Shannon: I SHANNON, TAKE YOU ROBERT, TO BE NO OTHER THAN YOURSELF. LOVING WHAT I KNOW OF YOU, TRUSTING WHAT I DO NOT YET KNOW. WITH RESPECT FOR YOUR INTEGRITY, AND FAITH IN YOUR LOVE FOR ME, THROUGH ALL OUR YEARS AND IN ALL THAT LIFE MAY BRING US, THROUGH THE BEST AND THE WORST, I WILL LOVE YOU FAITHFULLY.

The ceremony did not include any readings or poetry but did have a wine cup ceremony. (For more on the wine cup ceremony, see page 56.) "We did this in lieu of the now-traditional unity candle lighting and in lieu of the increasingly popular rose ceremony," says Shannon. "We felt the wine cup ceremony represented our relationship and hopes better."

Following the ceremony, the couple then embraced their guests before walking down the aisle. "We turned to our friends and family and hugged [them] and thanked them for coming. It was that closeness and intimacy we were striving for. No, it wasn't traditional, but it was us in every way," says Shannon.

CEREMONIES WITHIN CEREMONIES

Whether you choose to write your vows or use the old favorites, you have other ways to make your ceremony special.

UNITY CANDLE CEREMONY

One of the more popular ceremonial touches is the lighting of the unity candle, which can be done in a variety of ways. One of the more popular versions is as follows: The mothers of the bride and groom each light one taper candle at the front of the church. This usually happens just before they are seated. Once vows and rings are exchanged, the officiant explains the significance of the candles. The bride and groom each take one of the two candles that represents their individual lives and use the flames to light a third, symbolizing their oneness as husband and wife.

This activity need not be limited to the bride and groom. The couple can have their parents, grandparents, friends, children, and any other special people join in the lighting of the unity candle.

ROSE CEREMONY

During the rose ceremony, which has been gaining in popularity, the bride and groom exchange roses as first gifts to one another. This usually occurs after the couple has been pronounced husband and wife.

During Keely and Xan's rose ceremony, the minister spoke about the rose being a symbol of love. He asked the couple to always remember the significance of the red rose. "It is our wish that wherever you make your home there be special place in it for red roses and that on each anniversary of this special occasion you celebrate it, at least in part, by each of you bringing to that special place a red rose," he said. He also spoke about the difficulties of marriage and how the red rose can be used to remind one another to always come back to love.

Following the ceremony, the bride and groom gave the roses to the new mothers-in-law. "It was a wonderful way to end our ceremony," says Keely.

WINE CUP CEREMONY

During their wedding, Shannon and Robert had a wine cup ceremony to symbolize their willingness to share in both the joys and the disappointments of life. According to Shannon, the wine cup ceremony was a way for the couple to express their view of their future together. "We knew there would be difficulties mixed in with the good, and we were affirming to ourselves and our friends that we knew this and were taking this step together," says Shannon.

For this ritual, which took place before the couple was pronounced husband and wife, each of them drank from a cup filled with wine. Shannon found the words for the ceremony on UltimateWedding.com. (Go to www.weddingromance.com/poems. Select Vows and Ceremonies, then select Wine Ceremony.) "We felt that the words . . . reflected who we are and what our expectations of life are. We also felt that this ceremony had not been 'overdone' like so many of the new rituals at weddings," says Shannon.

OTHER RITUALS

You can use other rituals to personalize your ceremony. The **water ceremony**, where the bride and groom each pour a vessel of water into one container to symbolize their union, is an alternative to the unity candle ceremony. The **sand ceremony** substitutes sand for the water. (See page 58 to read about Christina and Neal's sand ceremony.) Couples who have children might consider the **family medallion ceremony** (see page 168).

If you choose one of these rituals, feel free to modify it to further suit you. You can even start from scratch and create your own.

COMBINING CULTURES OR RELIGIONS

Tying the knot can be more complicated when two cultures or religions are involved—even if the wedding will be small. Because each culture and religion has its own set of wedding rituals and expectations, mixed couples can be challenged when combining their beliefs and fitting them into one wedding.

For instance, if the bride is a devout Christian and the groom practices Judaism, the couple must decide if and how they want to incorporate rituals and readings from both religions into the wedding.

Ellen, who is Christian, and Chris, who is Jewish, had both a priest and a rabbi officiate at their intimate ceremony at an estate in New Jersey. Because both religions were important to the couple, they chose different elements from each religion and brought them together. They had readings from both religions and included both Christian and Jewish rituals, such as the lighting of the unity candle (primarily Christian) and the breaking of the glass (Jewish). "The ceremony was very unique," says Ellen.

Linda and Evan, on the other hand, decided to have a judge preside over their inter-faith ceremony at a hotel in Pittsburgh, Pennsylvania. "Neither Evan [Jewish] nor I [Presbyterian] attend [worship] regularly, so we didn't feel comfortable having to choose between a church or a synagogue. We also felt that it would be easier on our families to find neutral ground," explains Linda. Like Ellen and Chris, the couple combined readings and rituals from both religions to create a ceremony that was unique. "We chose to evenly represent our faiths and our individual likes," says Linda.

did *you* know?

Ethnic customs are used in 15 percent of weddings.

[source: Hallmark Press Room (http://pressroom.hallmark.com)]

Even when a couple decides to fairly represent both religions, like Linda and Evan did, they may still face opposition from family members who don't agree with their plans. Evan's brother, for instance, who is an Orthodox Jew, wouldn't attend the wedding because of the mixed religions.

While some family members might not come around, others might feel more comfortable with your plans if you involve them in the ceremony to contribute something from their own religion.

Despite the challenges mixed or interfaith couples face, a wedding that combines both the bride's and groom's cultural or religious backgrounds is a true celebration of that couple. It shows that the couple accepts one another's beliefs, however different, and

LOOKING FOR AN OFFICIANT?

If you are an interfaith couple looking for someone to marry you, check out Interfaith.org (www.interfaith.org/referrals). If you need a rabbi, consult the Rabbinic Center for Research and Counseling (www.rcrconline.org), which offers (for a fee) a list of rabbis who will officiate at interfaith ceremonies.

emphasizes their willingness to create a future that celebrates those differences.

Not all couples feel the need to have their cultural or religious background play a role in their wedding. In some instances, the bride might be adamant about including her religion in the ceremony while the groom does not feel that way about his. In others, neither the bride nor the groom wants to include specific cultural or religious elements—planning that kind of ceremony is a simpler task.

SEVEN QUESTIONS TO ANSWER FOR AN INTERFAITH CEREMONY:

1. Will the ceremony be performed on "neutral ground"?
2. Will we have a nondenominational minister, a judge, or officiants from both faiths?
3. How can we include family members so that they will feel more comfortable with the idea?
4. What readings will we choose so that both faiths are equally represented?
5. Will we include music from both faiths?
6. Will we create a wedding program explaining each of the wedding rituals and customs so that our guests can better understand the interfaith service?
7. If portions of our service are not in our common language, will we have a translator?

A Chinese Tea Ceremony

CHRISTINA AND NEAL wanted a ceremony by the lake for their intimate June wedding. An open-air courtyard at the Fuller Museum of Art in Brockton, Massachusetts, was a perfect fit.

Although Christina is of Chinese descent, she didn't want a traditional Chinese wedding. "Most Chinese weddings are extremely elaborate with huge Chinese banquets of about 500 to 750 people.... [There] tend[s] to be lots of drinking, playing mahjong, and teasing the couple with embarrassing games and tricks," she explains. This definitely didn't suit her style. Besides, most of her friends and relatives as well as the majority of Neal's relatives live in Asia. A small wedding with just immediate family seemed appropriate.

Because Christina and Neal invited only eighteen guests, the couple was able to cover the cost of airline tickets and accommodations for the five guests that flew in from Singapore for the event.

The couple put a great deal of thought into planning the wedding. Everything from the invitations to the centerpieces reflected a modern, chic sense of style. The most important feature, however, was the ceremony.

Because of their Asian background, the couple incorporated elements of their culture into their afternoon nuptials. Along with traditional Western vows performed in English by a nondenominational Protestant minister, the couple recited their vows in Chinese. But what made their ceremony truly special was the inclusion of a Chinese tea ceremony.

Christina explains that during a Chinese tea ceremony, also performed on other special occasions, younger members of the family serve tea to the elders as a form of respect. During a wedding, the bride and groom serve tea to their parents, grandparents, aunts, and uncles. After drinking the tea, the elders give the couple their blessings and red packets containing money. "Usually the bride will wear something red during the ceremony, as red is an auspicious color. Thus, I changed from my white wedding dress into a red chiffon dress for the ceremony," says Christina.

To make the ceremony even more meaningful, Christina and Neal used the teapot and teacup set that Christina's mother and father used when they were married thirty-one years earlier.

The couple thought the outdoor wedding would be too windy for lighting a unity candle, so instead they had a sand ceremony. Each of them poured sand from a pail into a single glass jar to represent their union. They used sand collected from the Namibia Sand Dunes during the couple's six-month vacation to the region. Christina adds that for her the sand ceremony was the highlight of the wedding ceremony.

GET WITH THE PROGRAM

Offering your guests a wedding program so that they can follow along with your intimate ceremony is a nice touch. It keeps your guests informed, adds a personal touch to your ceremony, and makes a wonderful keepsake for the guests—and for you.

If your ceremony combines various religious traditions, a wedding program is a great way to explain to your guests what the various rituals mean: What's the significance of the chuppah, or bridal canopy, under which a Jewish ceremony takes place? What is the unity candle? What is the Chinese tea ceremony?

A standard, simple wedding program provides a chronological list of the parts of the service. It's no more than a few pages long and usually includes the following:

- names of the bride and groom
- time and date of the wedding
- order of events
- the couple's music selections
- the couple's chosen readings and/or poetry

WEDDING PROGRAM IDEAS

Looking for examples of wedding programs? Check out ForeverWed.com (www.foreverwed1.com/articles/programs/links.html).

⊛ names of the participants, including the musicians, officiants, attendants, and parents

⊛ explanations of various religious rituals used in an interfaith ceremony

Being a writer, I chose a more elaborate program. I wanted more than a list of events; I wanted to describe each person who had a role in the wedding and what they meant to Darin and me. I also wanted to thank everyone who helped with the wedding itself or the preparations and give them credit for their contributions. I also wanted to include a few love quotes that dazzled me. As a result, our wedding program (which I made using my computer) ended up being an eleven-page booklet.

Although you can have your programs printed by a professional, plenty of couples make their programs, like I did. All you need is a word processing program, some clip art, and quality paper. If you like, you can use ribbon to tie the pages together. A more elaborate wedding program can also include the following:

⊛ words of thanks to guests and wedding participants

⊛ brief biographies of everyone involved in the wedding, including their affiliation with the bride and groom

⊛ special quotes that are meaningful to the couple

⊛ directions to the reception

⊛ order of events for the reception

USING YOUR IMAGINATION

Some couples get really creative when it comes to wedding programs. If the wedding has a theme, that theme can influence the style of the program. For instance, a couple who is having a medieval wedding might use scrolls. For a Japanese wedding, the programs can be printed on paper fans. If the wedding has a garden theme, pressed flowers might be used to decorate the programs.

MORE WAYS TO MAKE YOUR WEDDING PROGRAM UNIQUE:

⊛ Include a story about how you met.

- ⊚ Include copies of the poems or readings used in the ceremony.

- ⊚ If you write your own vows, include the text.

- ⊚ Talk about the significance of the ceremony location. If it's a historical church, you might discuss its history within the community.

- ⊚ Include a photo of yourselves.

CAPTURING THE DAY ON FILM

One of the most important aspects of your wedding planning is how to document the ceremony. During the minutes your ceremony will last, you will create a storehouse of memories. Some will fade with time, so it's essential to have a photographer capture your special day on film, giving you a permanent record of those special moments.

In the years following your wedding, you'll enjoy perusing those photos. Someday you'll be able to share them with your children and grandchildren.

The quality of these photos can vary. Some couples are willing to scale down other aspects of their wedding just to pay for an excellent photographer. Other couples, however, have other priorities and might simply rely on friends and family to photograph the event.

TIPS FOR CHOOSING A PROFESSIONAL PHOTOGRAPHER:

- ⊚ Start early. Good photographers book up fast.

- ⊚ Look for a good rapport between you and the photographer. You might want to shop around until you find that. You'll be spending the entire day with him, so it will help if you don't find him entirely obnoxious.

- ⊚ Ask the photographer for references, then call them.

- ⊚ Preview a wide variety of the photographer's work.

- ⊚ Find out whether the photographer you speak with will actually photograph your wedding. Some companies have several photographers and will send out whoever is available.

- ⊚ Make sure you are clear about the photographer's prices and that there aren't any hidden costs.

☙ Ask how the photographs will be finished. Your finished pictures should look different than your raw proofs.

Keep in mind that not all churches allow photographs during a wedding ceremony. Ask the officiant what the rules are, and discuss them with your photographer beforehand. You might have to reenact some ceremony elements in order to get pictures of them.

PHOTOGRAPHY TRENDS

Black-and-white photos, as well as photos in sepia tones may still be all the rage, but I like the idea of having some photos in color. Darin and I ordered equal numbers of black-and-white and color photos.

Another popular trend is photojournalistic or candid shots. Despite the name, many "candid" shots are actually set up by the photographer. These shots might include the bride leaning over to kiss her grandmother, the flower girl reaching up to hug the bride, or the bride and groom laughing together.

FINDING A PHOTOGRAPHER

If you're looking for a professional photographer in your area, check out www.ppa.com. It lists photographers who are members of the Professional Photographers of America.

A great candid shot—especially one that's actually candid—can be quite special. Unfortunately, our photographer wasn't into the photojournalistic style, so almost all of our wedding photographs were posed. Our friends and family, however, managed to capture a few great unposed moments on film, and those pictures are some of my favorites.

Another trend, digital photography, can transform photos into works of art. Some photographers use digital cameras to take wedding photos; others use traditional 35mm cameras and convert the pictures to digital format via computer. If you are interested in this format, you should have no trouble finding photographers who specialize in this high-tech medium.

SHOOTING THE CEREMONY

If you get married in a church or other house of worship, your photographer might not be allowed to capture the ceremony itself on film because of church rules. After the service you and your sweetie might have to reenact the event for the photographer.

Whether or not this is the case, it's a good idea to give the photographer a list of photos that you want—and those you don't want—and do so well before the big day. Maybe it's really important to you to have your first kiss as husband and wife captured on film. Let the photographer know. Maybe you want some photos of the guests. Maybe you'd like a close-up of your husband as he says his vows. Be clear about your preferences. Some couples even see photos that they like in books or magazines and show them to the photographer beforehand.

Because your ceremony will be small, you can have pictures taken of everyone there. Some couples have the photographer take a photo of the entire group just following the ceremony. Others have the photographer take pictures of friends and family members who have no official role in the wedding but mean a great deal to the couple. Once again, it's important to inform your photographer whom you would like her to photograph. Several couples I interviewed failed to give the photographer a list of preferred shots, and they ended up disappointed.

CEREMONY SHOT LIST

This list includes some traditional and not-so-traditional photo ideas.

Before the ceremony:

- Bride getting ready
- Bride with parents
- Bride with attendants
- Bride leaving for ceremony
- Groom with parents
- Groom with attendants

During the ceremony:

- Groom at altar waiting for bride
- Bride walking down aisle
- Ring exchange
- Kiss at altar
- Close-up of parents during ceremony
- Wedding party at altar
- Interior of church during ceremony (shows all of your guests)
- Bride and groom walking down aisle
- Couple walking out of the church
- Couple accepting congratulations after the ceremony

After the ceremony:

- Bride and groom
- Bride and groom with bride's family
- Bride and groom with groom's family
- Bride and groom with both families
- Bride and groom with attendants

PICTURES BEFORE THE CEREMONY

If you don't want your guests mulling about after the ceremony, waiting for you to have your pictures taken, you can arrange to have the photos of you and your sweetie taken beforehand.

For couples who want to adhere to tradition, many photographs can still be taken before the ceremony. Posed portraits of the bridal party and the family can be done in advance as long as they include the bride or the groom, but not both.

CAUGHT ON TAPE

Darin and I didn't feel it was necessary to videotape our wedding—but we changed our minds at the last minute. A few days before our wedding, we decided to have a friend tape the wedding with our video camera.

Although our friend got the ceremony taped (we're so glad he did!), he failed to capture the important moments of the reception because the video recorder's batteries died. Neither Darin nor I had bothered to check the batteries beforehand.

Although we don't regret having an amateur video of our event, several couples I interviewed said that, in hindsight, they would have hired a professional videographer. "I would have paid to have a videographer. It was left in a family member's hands, and we ended up with no video of the day! Very disappointing!" says one bride.

When searching for a videographer, ask many of the same questions you would ask a photographer. Also, make sure you see plenty of work samples.

If you decide to ask a friend or family member to tape the wedding, tell her what you'd like to have on the video—and what you don't want. Also, make sure she has fully charged batteries in the video camera!

© 2003 LEE KROHN

A Vermont Ceremony by Candlelight

~

NICOLE & NED

SOUTH LONDONDERRY, VERMONT

THE MEETING:	The couple, who reside in Westport, Connecticut, met on a blind date at a birthday celebration that both had been invited to. Interestingly, both almost backed out of the date.
THE PROPOSAL:	Ned proposed to Nicole during a surprise weekend getaway. After a romantic dinner at a fancy restaurant, the two took a walk along the oceanside boardwalk. "He proceeded to tell me all these wonderful things about why he loved me and that he wanted to give me a token of his love. He then asked me to marry him," says Nicole.
CEREMONY:	Old town hall building, South Londonderry, Vermont
RECEPTION:	Three Clock Inn, South Londonderry, Vermont
NUMBER OF GUESTS:	52
COST:	$16,115; paid for by the couple
PLANNING DURATION:	9 months

Nicole knew early on that she wanted a small wedding. She had attended an intimate wedding several years before, and it made a big impact on her. "I loved the fact that [the couple] got to meet all the guests and [the guests] really got to hang out with the bride and groom," she says.

Vermont seemed like the perfect wedding location. Nicole's family owned a second home in Vermont where she and Ned, both avid skiers, enjoyed visiting. Having the wedding in Vermont also meant the couple could scale down the size because they wouldn't feel pressured to invite everyone they knew.

Another factor in their decision to have fewer guests was money. Nicole and Ned put the additional money they would have had to spend on a big wedding toward a trip around the world. "Our wedding wasn't about the perfect flowers, the perfect first song, the tablecloth colors, the bridesmaids' dresses. It wasn't about perfection, color schemes, or anything like that.... It was about everyone there expressing their love," Nicole says.

NEW ENGLAND CHARM

Spending time with each of their wedding guests was a high priority for Nicole and Ned, so they planned an entire weekend of activities—with the wedding ceremony as the climax. The wedding weekend began with a rehearsal dinner at Nicole's mother's ten-acre country home in Vermont, and everyone on the wedding guest list was invited. "We had a casual buffet dinner with tons of food and a fire pit in the backyard so that people could roast marshmallows and listen to the river behind the house," says Nicole.

At 6 P.M. the following day, the couple's immediate family gathered at South Londonderry's old town hall building, the ceremony site, for photographs.

Even though Ned was raised Episcopalian and Nicole was raised Catholic, the couple decided to have their ceremony at the old town hall rather than a church. "[The town hall] looks more like an old-fashioned schoolhouse.... It is very rustic and simple," Nicole says.

A florist transformed the room they used with candles, trees, and flowers into what Nicole calls "a magnificent, magical indoor garden." She says, "It looked like a garden from *A Midsummer Night's Dream*. It was exquisite."

THE CEREMONY

At 7 P.M., the remainder of the guests arrived at the old town hall. Many of them were surprised to discover that a cocktail hour preceded the ceremony. After sipping beverages and nibbling on appetizers, the guests were asked to momentarily leave the room so it could be prepared for the ceremony.

When the guests returned, each was handed a small candle and escorted by a lantern-bearing groomsman to the altar, where they lit another candle and offered a prayer or kind wishes for the couple. Each guest then sat in one of the chairs that formed a diamond shape around the altar.

Nicole says that when all of the nearly two hundred candles were lit, they bathed the room in soft light. Besides the candles at the altar, there were candles on the floor, hanging from the ceiling, dangling from chairs, and adorning ten-foot (3 meters) birch trees that had been brought in for the wedding. Some guests also held candles during the ceremony. "There was absolutely no unnatural light anywhere in the building," says Nicole.

Aside from aesthetic appeal, the candles provided symbolism. "I liked the symbolism. We wanted the guests to be involved, and we wanted each guest to have taken the moment to think of kind wishes and prayers for us as they lit their candles," explains Nicole.

"I DO"

Nicole chose to walk down the aisle alone. When she arrived at the altar, she and Ned, who had been waiting for her there, each lit a candle.

The justice of the peace offered his opening remarks, and a groomsman read a poem called "Love's Philosophy" by Percy Bysshe Shelley. After a sermon about marriage, one of Nicole's two maids of honor read the poem "How Do I Love Thee?" by Elizabeth Barrett Browning. Nicole and Ned exchanged traditional wedding vows. "Our wedding was so nontraditional; it was nice to have something that was traditional," says Nicole.

Following the vows, Nicole's best friend recited a love poem that Nicole had written for Ned. "This supposedly made everyone including the men cry," says Nicole.

The couple then exchanged rings, and a poem that Ned's great-grandfather had written was recited. Prayers followed.

Once the couple was pronounced husband and wife, they had their first dance—in the aisle. "We have no idea what we actually danced to except that it was a waltz," says Nicole. A string trio had provided the music.

After the ceremony, guests headed next door to The Three Clock Inn, a high-end French restaurant, for a formal five-course meal. Cocktails followed in the couple's hotel room. The next morning, the wedding guests had an opportunity to bond at a brunch at a local restaurant.

Nicole says she and Ned created "one of the most beautiful settings" she had ever seen for their wedding. "I doubt anyone will ever confuse my wedding with anyone else's or, for that matter, forget it.... I go to parties now and people say, 'You are the one who had that ceremony? We heard all about how beautiful it was,'" she says.

BRIDE TO BRIDE

- Be prepared that some uninvited people might be offended. If you don't want to deal with offending someone, you might want to consider having a larger wedding.

- Be aware a small wedding doesn't necessarily require less planning than a large wedding.

- Get your guests involved in the ceremony through readings, prayers, etc. Find a way to include everyone.

Nicole

Nicole and Ned's Wedding Budget

Reception venue, food, and beverages	$8,000
(The couple had no wedding cake or music at the reception.)	
Attire	$125
(This amount is for the rental tux.	
The gown was a gift to Nicole from her mother.)	
Flowers	$1,700
Photography	$1,200
Stationery	$100
Gifts	$390
Wedding rings	$3,900
Ceremony	$700
Total	**$16,115**

CHAPTER 5

A Reception to Remember

The ceremony's over. You are officially husband and wife. It's time to celebrate!

Perhaps you and your handful of guests will enjoy a quiet dinner at a fabulous restaurant, or maybe you'll transform your parents' backyard into "party central" and dance the night away with family and friends.

Because you are having a small wedding, you can think outside the box when planning your reception. You won't need as much space as you would for a larger wedding, so you can choose from a wider variety of locations. Your reception won't necessarily adhere to tradition. Skip the electric slide, the garter toss, and the clinking glasses, if you choose, and throw in some rituals of your own.

LAVISH OR LOW KEY?

For your reception, one of the first choices you need to make is whether the event will be formal or casual. You might picture an elegant soiree, complete with a jazz band, fine wines, gourmet food, and an extravagant setting. Conversely, you might prefer an outdoor picnic potluck where comfortable summer attire is appropriate.

You'll also have to choose the time of day and type of meal for your reception. Will you have a plated dinner or a brunch buffet?

BRUNCH AND LUNCH

Several couples I interviewed opted for a brunch buffet or luncheon instead of an evening meal, and holding a reception earlier in the day has several advantages.

One of the biggest is cost. A morning or midday meal is usually significantly less expensive than an evening one. Your guests aren't likely to drink as much as they would at an evening reception. If you choose to serve alcohol, only wine and champagne are necessary, although some couples choose to have an open bar with mixed drinks available.

SERVING SPIRITS?

Need to know how much wine to purchase for your wedding? Rule of thumb is one-third of a bottle of wine for each person for lunch and one-half a bottle per person for dinner or a wine and cheese function. To learn more, check out the party calculator at www.moneycops.com.

Venue availability is also a benefit. You might have a better chance finding an opening at a popular venue if your reception will be early in the day.

Another advantage is that an early reception is generally shorter than a later reception. Some couples prefer this to a drawn-out evening event.

Jan and Mike wanted a simple reception, without dancing, so they chose to host a luncheon at a restaurant that is a converted train car. "I have always [avoided] the limelight. [I] never enjoyed big weddings . . . with all the protocol, receiving lines, etc. . . . I wanted to feel relaxed but still wanted to be the bride," says Jan.

Because of Jan's love of trains, the café they chose was a perfect fit. "I wanted something different. I have been to so many horrible weddings in legion halls. . . . I wanted people to have a decent lunch," says Jan, noting that they chose a buffet of hot chicken, salads, cheeses, and fruit.

If you have an earlier reception, you can still make it elegant. Lynette and Charles, who got married in December inside a Phoenix mansion, had an elaborate reception with brunch that included—among many other choices—iced jumbo shrimp, a carving station with prime rib, an omelet station, and eggs Benedict. The couple did not want dancing at their reception, so they had Christmas carolers as well as a harpist provide the music for the afternoon. They also decided to forgo the bouquet toss and the garter toss. "We wanted to make our day more memorable with the carolers and harp, [not] bore the guests with the typical reception activities," says Lynette. (For more on Lynette and Charles's wedding, see page 130.)

A COCKTAIL RECEPTION

White linen. Plates of scrumptious appetizers. Ice sculptures. Fruit displays. Gerbera daisies. Swanky jazz tunes. Wine. Tuxedos and gowns. A cocktail reception can be a sophisticated, yet less expensive alternative to a dinner event. Along with cost, many of the same advantages of a lunch or brunch reception apply for a cocktail reception. It doesn't usually last as long as a dinner, which can be good for couples who want to make their getaway sooner rather than later. It can have all the same rituals of a traditional wedding reception or none at all. Although many cocktail receptions are somewhat formal, they don't have to be. (One drawback, however, is that your guests might indulge a bit more on alcohol.) Usually a cocktail reception has no assigned table seating. Guests tend to stand and mingle.

Jane and Mike had a cocktail reception at a California inn rather than a sit-down meal. "We had appetizers and wine and [other] beverages with circulating waiters," says Jane, who says the food was "practically cheap!" She describes the reception as "bright, summery, festive, informal, [and] flowery."

JUST DESSERTS

Imagine tables full of desserts: three of your favorite kinds of cheesecake, some mocha and chocolate tortes, freshly baked pies, pastries, handmade chocolates, homemade cookies, and five kinds of ice cream. I don't know about you, but that sounds like my kind of reception.

A dessert reception, which can be held in the afternoon or evening, is a mouthwatering and flexible option. Dessert can be passed around by servers or placed on a buffet table. Although champagne and wine make nice accompaniments, they are not necessary. Couples who don't want alcohol at their reception might choose to serve tea and coffee. Just like the cocktail reception, this delicious event is usually

CHOCOLATE DECOR

Instead of an ice sculpture at your wedding, how about a chocolate sculpture? Check out www.nhwedding.com/eatonschocolates/candy.html. Available items include a chocolate basket and a chocolate swan. A chocolate fountain (see www.thechocolatefountain.com) lets guests dip fruit or other treats into melted chocolate.

short but sweet, and it is less structured than a dinner reception. One thing to keep in mind: If you have diabetics on the guest list, make sure you provide some sugar-free options.

DINNER: BUFFET VS. SIT-DOWN STYLE

Dinner receptions generally last longer than other receptions. If you want to spend several hours celebrating with your guests, dinner is the way to go. Some couples extend the evening by having toasts, dancing, a cake cutting, and other wedding-day rituals. Others, especially those having only a handful of guests, treat it more like a get-together among friends and family.

If you want a dinner reception, you'll have to decide whether you want a buffet or a sit-down meal. For an intimate wedding, either option can work.

Having guests serve themselves can be a fun way to get everyone up and mingling. Buffet meals tend to be less formal than sit-down dinners, making buffets a great option for couples who want a reception with a more casual feel. Buffets can also be less expensive than sit-down dinners, but that depends on the menu you choose.

SPECIAL DIETS

Find out beforehand if any of your guests have special food needs. If there are vegetarians in the group, have meat-free choices. If there are diabetics in the group, have some sugar-free dessert options.

The majority of couples I interviewed had a sit-down meal. For Kerry and John, having a small guest list allowed them to splurge and give their guests a fine dining experience. "Unless we wanted to go into debt—we didn't—we could afford a pasta buffet and limited bar for two hundred, or [we could] serve a seated meal of filet mignon and host an open bar all night for fewer and still save quite a bit! We felt that while the ceremony was for us, the reception was where we wanted to spoil our guests a little, thanking them for their love and support," says Kerry.

Although most couples have either a restaurant or caterer provide the meal, some couples have their family members provide the food. If the couples are really ambitious, they cook the meal themselves. Therese and James, who had their reception at a relative's home, cooked a feast for their sixteen guests. The reception was a fun and informal family get-together with plenty of laughing and dancing. "We cooked and hosted a four-course dinner for our family, all the food in Italian style, and we sat and ate and drank and talked and laughed for hours," says Therese. "There was one moment when my husband and I were sitting head to head holding hands looking at everyone talking and having a good time, and we agreed that everything worked out perfectly because we were having a great time and so was everyone else."

A Tea Party Reception

REBECCA AND LEE, who reside in Florida, wanted a simple, stress-free wedding. They didn't want a receiving line or a fancy sit-down meal, complete with speeches and dancing, or any adult attendants. They simply wanted to get married while surrounded by people they loved.

The couple found a bridal shop in Rebecca's hometown of Searcy, Arkansas, that was perfect for the occasion. The rose garden situated beside the shop was an ideal place for their "I dos," and a room inside—complete with a fireplace and piano—would hold all of their thirty-five guests for the reception.

The couple's outdoor ceremony, which was held in the afternoon, involved only family. "My brother-in-law conducted the ceremony, but my father, who is a preacher, actually married us," says Rebecca.

Following the ceremony, invited guests joined them inside the bridal shop for a "tea reception," where they enjoyed finger foods (small cheesecakes, spinach wraps, ham puffs, small sandwiches, and sausages), most of which Rebecca's mother made, and wedding cake. Piano music accompanied the event.

In keeping with the tea party theme, teapots decorated the serving tables, and saucers and teacups holding daisies were the centerpieces. Mismatched tablecloths with lace overlays covered each table. "Some of the tablecloths were my mom's, some were my sister's, and some were from garage sales. They had a very cozy, simple elegance about them," says Rebecca.

The couple added other personal touches to the reception, including handmade picture boards that showed photographs of them at various stages in their lives. They also paid a special tribute to the men in their families who were part of the military. (The U.S. was at war with Iraq at the time of their wedding.) "[Lee] is a [former] marine, my father is a [retired] air force man and [Lee's] father was also in the air force, so we had 8 x 10 pictures of all three of them in uniform placed on the picture table.... I think it meant a lot to our fathers for us to show everyone how proud we are of their military service," says Rebecca.

THE RECEIVING LINE: IS IT NECESSARY?

One of my pet peeves about large weddings is the receiving line. I recently went to a wedding where I had to stand in line for twenty minutes to greet the bride and groom—not my idea of a good time. That said, I do realize the necessity of having a receiving line at a large wedding so that the bride and groom can have one-on-one time with their guests.

A receiving line for a small wedding is different. It's obviously smaller, and because of its size, it's usually less rushed. Therese and Mark, who had thirty guests at their wedding, regret not having a receiving line. "I didn't think one would be needed with only thirty guests (and six of those guests were in the wedding party!). But people expect one, and there's a bit of confusion if you don't have one," says Therese.

Darin and I didn't want a receiving line at our wedding, and no one seemed confused by our decision. We tried to mingle with as many guests as we could during the cocktail hour. If you choose to omit the receiving line, make sure you and your new spouse take the time to greet everyone. Before you plunk down, cocktail in hand, on a comfy chair—after all those pictures, you'll be looking forward to that moment!—grab your partner and make your rounds. If you really must sit back and relax first, visit each table after dinner is over. You can even serve the wedding cake and visit with your guests as you do so.

SEATING FOR YOU AND YOUR GUESTS

Darin and I did not want to have a head table and be set apart from everyone else. We didn't want to feel like we were on display. Instead, we sat with our parents and our honor attendants at a round table inside the tent, which worked wonderfully. We had a perfect view of all our guests without feeling like we were onstage.

Seating is another advantage of a small wedding: You can be flexible with the arrangements. If you want a head table, go for it, but you have other options. You can have a sweetheart table for just the two of you. You can do what Darin and I did. You can sit with your entire immediate family. You might even be able to seat everyone at one table.

Kerry and John chose to sit at a sweetheart table in the middle of the room. "The other tables formed a circle around us. There were eighty-eight chairs for sixty-four people so

DONATE YOUR LEFTOVERS

If you have food left over from the reception, consider donating it to a local food bank or shelter. Contact America's Second Harvest (www.secondharvest.org) for more information.

that people could get up from their own table and sit down at another to talk if they wanted," says Kerry. "It was a great feeling to be surrounded by our families and friends, and I recommend it all the time to friends planning weddings."

Elle and Rory also used a sweetheart table for their wedding, which had twenty-eight guests. "We entered the reception to a round of applause and were guided by our bridal party up to our sweetheart table. . . . People came up and took photos of us. We felt like movie stars!" says Elle.

Elle says a sweetheart table is perfect for an intimate wedding—especially if the couple has several attendants. "[It's] something I fully recommend for a small wedding; otherwise, half the people will be up front with you [at the head table]," she says.

If you'll have only a handful of guests at your wedding, you can have everyone sit at one table, like Shannon and Robert did for their eight-guest wedding. "The entire evening felt as though we had just had our friends over for dinner. It was truly amazing," says Shannon.

Although you don't need assigned seating for a small party, many couples use assigned seating for their intimate weddings. It prevents confusion for guests, and it can be a nice way for people who might not otherwise sit together to get to know one another.

YOU CAN DANCE IF YOU WANT TO

Some couples can't imagine a wedding reception without dancing. For them, it's part of the celebration. Others—like Darin and me—would rather pass on this option. It's not that we don't like moving to our favorite tunes. We just didn't want to feel pressured to occupy the dance floor at our wedding.

I found in the couples I interviewed quite an even split between those who chose to have dancing and those who did not. Some couples liked that a small wedding relieved the pressure to include dancing. Despite their small weddings, other couples felt almost obligated to make dancing part of the reception. Still others not only loved the idea of having a dance floor but also took dance lessons to prepare.

Linda and Robert, who had fifty-five people at their estate wedding, are a case in point. "My husband and I had taken a few lessons," says Linda. "Just being out there dancing with my new husband, family, and closest friends was such a thrill. I really didn't want the night to end."

Karen and Robert, who got married at an estate, had family give them some pointers. "[Robert's] parents had come up to our house a few weeks prior to the wedding to give us some dance lessons. We didn't do great with the lessons, but we had always managed to dance pretty well together in the past," says Karen. However, Karen admits being a bit nervous about getting her moves just right. "I got a little bit worried about flubbing the dance thing in front of all of our guests, but when we were in each other's arms and dancing (and we did very well!) it didn't matter."

Nancy and Jose spent several months getting ready for their first dance. "We had been learning, choreographing, and practicing for over two months, and boy, was I nervous; but it went all smooth," says Nancy.

Linda and Evan, on the other hand, left their dancing shoes at home. "Our reception was quite simple: a very nice dinner, but no dancing," says Linda. "Our crowd was pretty tame, as we are in our thirties and not much interested in club dancing and drinking to extinction anymore. . . . Everyone just mingled and talked and laughed."

Amie and Dan, who had fifty-three guests at their reception at a family member's home, had a simple reception without dancing. "We didn't have a deejay or band, just some light music on a sound system that went through the house and also on the porch. People mostly just wandered through the house, mingled, and ate," says Amie.

If you want to have dancing at your reception but feel that your small wedding will make it more difficult to fill up the dance floor, don't fret. There are ways to encourage your guests to kick up their heels:

- **Lead the way**. If you and your sweetie are out there having a good time, others are likely to follow your lead.

- **Let your fun-loving friends and family get everyone moving**. If you have a friend or a family member who gets right into the party spirit, have her accompany the two of you on the dance floor. When your guests see all of you having a good time, they might feel compelled to join you.

- **Make time for dancing**. Make sure your meal is served on time and that speeches don't run too long; otherwise, you might not have time to dance.

- **Mix it up**. Mix up the tunes a bit so you have songs that your guests will enjoy. Although you might not enjoy the latest dance hit, it might get your guests out of their chairs.

- **Set the mood**. Expecting your guests to boogie down under bright lights is a bit much to ask. People are much more inclined to dance in a place where the lighting is dim.

TOASTS AND SPEECHES

Does the thought of speaking at your wedding reception make you want to run and hide? Do you feel pressured to give a speech? If so, then you are just like I was a week before my wedding.

I had written a short poem for Darin. I knew I would be nervous, but I made a pact with myself that no matter what I was going to get to that microphone and read it. Even though the crowd was fairly small, I felt my heart pound as I stood and recited my poem. I'm so glad I didn't back down; it was one of the highlights of my evening.

If you suffer from stage fright, don't pressure yourself to recite a long speech. Saying just a few words is okay. If you are truly petrified of making a speech, don't do it. You can always write something meaningful and give it to your sweetie privately. As far as thanking your guests, you can simply let your new spouse do the honors while you stand side by side. If you both suffer from stage fright, ask the emcee to say your thank-yous on your behalf.

While you might not have stage fright, your wedding party might. Your maid of honor, for instance, might not feel comfortable giving a speech. Don't take it personally, and don't force her to speak.

At some weddings everyone seems to enjoy the limelight—so much so that the speeches drag on well into the night. If you want to keep the speaking short, it's a good idea to ask anyone who makes a toast or speech to do so within a time limit (three minutes is standard).

The speeches can be one of the most entertaining aspects of the reception. In fact, many of the brides I interviewed cited the toasts and speeches as being the highlight of their receptions.

For Linda and Mickey, who had nine guests at their wedding, a toast given by their young daughter stole the show. Just after everyone received their dinners, she decided to surprise her parents and make a toast. "She was so elegant, so amazing," says Linda. "[Her] speech was by far the highlight."

Ellen's favorite reception moment was her husband's speech. "[Chris] gave a very moving speech, and I wasn't the only one who was crying," she says.

WEDDING RITUALS OLD AND NEW

Having an intimate wedding means you'll have more freedom to exclude rituals that you don't feel are necessary, and the smaller the wedding, the greater that freedom to break with tradition. For instance, a garter toss would seem odd at a wedding with eight guests. A bouquet toss might also seem out of place.

Instead of including the standard rituals, you might have each of your guests share a favorite memory of you both or offer words of inspiration. Some couples find even more creative ways to entertain their guests during the reception.

During dinner, Misty and Michael's videographer played a photomontage that included pictures of both of them growing up, as well as photos of the couple during their dating years. They also played a seven-minute movie skit that they had filmed earlier with their videographer's help. "It was a comedy with a lot of cheesy, dramatic scenes, and it had everyone rolling with laughter. Embarrassing as it was, it was a hit!" says Misty.

Therese and Mark also played a video montage during their bed-and-breakfast reception. "The head of the audio-video department of a local community college did the video for us for a hundred dollars. He did a great job, and it was worth every penny! . . . There were three songs. The first song displayed photos of me growing up, the second song displayed photos of Mark, and the third segment, set to Martina McBride's song "Blessed," showed pictures of Mark and me and all of our family and friends who have come to mean so much to us. It was a nice way to incorporate those that have been important to us in our wedding," says Therese.

Carla and Todd, who had nine guests, decided to get their guests involved by creating a brand-new tradition. "I started my own tradition that anytime the bride claps her hands, everyone else had to kiss. Since I clap my hands every time I laugh, it made for an exciting and 'smoochy' evening," says Carla.

Not all couples choose to create their own rituals. Some stick with the tried and true. In fact, many couples I interviewed used the traditions of a standard large wedding despite the fact that their weddings were small.

Amie and Dan, for instance, said one highlight of their reception was the bouquet toss. "[It] was the best when Dan's grandma [widowed for several years] caught my bouquet," says Amie.

Linda and Roger, who had fifty-five guests at their wedding, had plenty of dancing (the electric slide, YMCA, and a conga line, among others), as well as bouquet and garter tosses. "The reception was exactly how I wanted because I wanted everyone to have fun and enjoy themselves—and they did! What started out as a peaceful, graceful wedding turned into a fun party," says Linda.

Maybe like Linda and Roger you have always wanted your big day to have all the typical wedding-day rituals. Maybe you'd rather have your reception feel like a casual dinner party without all the wedding-day hoopla. Either way, it's your day. Make it reflect what both of you want.

A Reception to Remember

MAGGIE AND OWEN's wedding was held in a huge, Victorian home in the center of a small town in New Brunswick, Canada. The home, which easily accommodated their sixty guests, has special meaning to the couple: Owen's grandmother owns it. "We approached her about using the home for our wedding, not sure if a woman of ninety years of age . . . would be up to the challenge it presented. She was elated. She and her husband had lived in that house since they got married sixty-five years before, and had raised their children there. She felt that celebrating a marriage would only add to the history of this old family home," explains Maggie.

After the 9 P.M. ceremony in the parlor, the reception—spread out among four rooms in the house—got rolling.

"We had hors d'oeuvres being served by Highland dancers in kilts [Maggie used to be a Highland dancer], as well as tables of munchies. An open bar manned by a bartender was located in the study. People milled around and mingled in the various rooms as music played in the background," Maggie says. A harpist played during the wedding ceremony as well as the first two hours of the reception, but they switched to rock/party music as midnight approached.

The entire home glowed with the warmth of five fireplaces that were aflame for the occasion. Dozens of poinsettias, which lined the home's grand staircase, also enhanced the festive mood.

The couple planned to have the wedding catered, but three days before the wedding the caterer cancelled due to illness. Luckily, the menu was hors d'oeuvres only, so the couple relied on their local grocery store for prepackaged hors d'oeuvres. "My mother, aunts, and family friends worked their butts off to ensure that I had food at my wedding. Although there was limited preparation, the ladies still worked through the wedding to ensure that the food was put into the oven, taken out of the oven, and given to the servers," says Maggie. "The food was delicious, and no one was the wiser."

The couple chose to skip the bouquet and garter tosses, but they did have a few speeches and toasts, including a champagne toast at midnight. "All of the guests gathered around to wish each other a happy new year and sing 'Auld Lang Syne,'" says Maggie.

SPECIAL TOUCHES

Simple things can make your wedding reception unique. Choosing unusual favors and place cards are just two easy ways you can add pizzazz to your intimate gathering. The smaller your wedding, the more you'll be able to splurge on these fun little details.

FAVORS

If you're the creative type and you have a bit of time before the big day, you can make your own favors, like I did. This is an ideal way to give the favors a personal touch and make sure they fit your wedding's theme.

Soap making is one of my favorite hobbies. My cupboards are filled with soap-making supplies, and nearly every room in our house has a basket full of soap. It seemed only natural to give my handmade bars as favors. Not only were they a representation of me; they fit perfectly for our garden wedding.

You can make your own edible wedding favors. Cookies wrapped in cellophane, jelly beans in a pretty jar, and homemade fudge pieces in cute boxes are just a few ideas.

If you're not inclined to make your own favors, you might turn to Internet resources. A wide variety of favors is just a click away.

You can't go wrong with edible favors—they won't end up collecting dust in someone's kitchen drawer! One of the coolest ideas I've found on the Web is personalized chocolate bar wrappers. The site at www.photowrappers.com offers candy bar wrappers that are personalized to include names, the wedding date, and even a photo. You can buy just the wrappers, or you can buy wrapped, brand-name chocolate bars. You can even buy personalized Lifesavers!

If you're having a beach wedding and you feel like splurging on the favors, check out www.giftfavors.com/themes/coolanduniquethmedfavors.html, which sells leis made from wrapped candy. These are colorful and truly unique.

At www.beau-coup.com/bestsellers.htm you can buy heart-shaped sugar cubes in glass tubes. Personalized mint tins are also available at this site.

For something edible and elegantly wrapped, look for French honey wrapped in white organza at www.splendidpalate.com/eventfavors.html. This site offers many other neat favors, including dried lavender bouquets and glassine-wrapped organic culinary lavender.

What about a photo of you and your sweetie? You can get the photo made out of chocolate and also framed in this decadent treat. Check out Coolpartystuff.com (www.coolpartystuff.com). Select the product category Chocolates.

If you want something utilitarian, check out www.giftfavors.com. Here you can find silver-plated bottle stoppers, chrome ice cream scoops, and chrome pizza cutters. Try www.adreamwedding.com for personalized cookie cutters in daisy, butterfly, or heart shapes. This site also offers bottled bath salts.

There are plenty of original favor ideas—a small terra-cotta pot of lavender or rosemary, samplers of gourmet coffee or herbal tea, a jar of homemade jam, or some decorative cocktail napkins, to name a few. Try to stick with something useful or consumable so your guests' memorabilia don't end up just collecting dust.

PLACE CARDS

Your choice of place cards can add a unique touch to your wedding reception. You can use them for seating purposes only, or you can attach them to favors so they double as gift tags. My sister-in-law glued pressed flowers onto watercolor paper and wrote the names with a black felt-tip pen to make fold-over place cards. They were perfect for our garden wedding.

Party Poofers (www.partypoofers.com/holders.htm) has place card holders in a variety of shapes, including stars, hearts, cherubs, and seashells. Not only are they neat ways to display your place cards, but they can double as favors.

Check out www.placetile.com for reusable handmade ceramic place cards. A special felt-tip marker (the marker's ink wipes off with a cloth) is provided to write the names of your guests. Another option is to hire a calligrapher for handwritten place cards. You can let the cards stand alone, or you can frame them so they'll also serve as favors.

What about edible place cards? Look at www.cookiesncream.com:8080/cookies.htm for hand-decorated cookie place cards. If you want to make your own cookie place card holders, see www.favoritebrandrecipes.com/Recipes/120/0918001120.htm. Chocolate place cards are available at www.sweetdistinction.com.

TABLE CARDS

For guests seating, you can simply number the tables, or do something unique and more imaginative. Darin and I named tables after our favorite paintings. We placed on each table a reproduction of its painting, labeled with the title and the artist.

Lynette and Charles named tables after Chicago landmarks. "We found greeting cards with old black-and-white photos of the landmarks and framed them in chunky gold frames to place on each table to identify where the guests would sit," says Lynette. "It was another way to tie the fact that we were living in Chicago and having our reception at the Wrigley [a mansion in Arizona], and it made for great conversation for the guests!"

Therese and Mark chose cartoon characters to mark the tables. "My husband loves WB cartoons. . . . Bugs Bunny is his favorite, so the head table was the Bugs Bunny table. The other tables were named Daffy Duck, Porky Pig, Foghorn Leghorn, Elmer Fudd, etc. Since I did most of the planning, this was a nice way to add a bit of [Mark's] personality to things," says Therese.

Suzette and Rich named tables for important events in their lives. "Guests [sat] at the 'Our First Date' table or 'The Proposal' table, etc.," says Suzette.

Other couples have incorporated their wedding theme into their table names or derived inspiration from favorite destinations, hobbies, or sports.

THE GUEST BOOK

Although you might opt for a traditional guest book, you can choose from many alternatives. Donna and Peter, who had a nautical-themed wedding, used a captain's log for their guest book. Darin and I had our guests sign a photo mat around our engagement photo. What about having guests sign on an unfired ceramic platter or bowl? Glaze and fire the bowl after the wedding for a treasured keepsake that's even functional!

Some of the couples I interviewed wanted more than just guest signatures. If you agree, you might appreciate their ideas.

Linda and Mickey used an instant camera to photograph each guest, then they mounted the photos in a guest book. Guests were encouraged to write messages by their photos. "[It was] very successful and lots of fun. We now have a picture of each of our guests [on our wedding day], along with their words of love, to cherish forever," says Linda.

Susan and Nikhil (featured on page 86) used as a guest book a scrapbook with pictures of themselves and of their guests. It was passed around at the wedding and all of the prewedding parties. "I have been to a lot of weddings where people get backed up behind the guest book and never sign it. I wanted to give all the guests . . . plenty of time to sign. Since the book had lots of blank pages, people could sign whatever and wherever they wanted. Some people just signed their name by a picture, but most wrote us very wonderful passages, poems, and well wishes," says Susan.

Pat and Chris used guest book sheets they found at the Guestbook Store (www.guest bookstore.com). This site offers a neat concept for couples who want more than just autographs from their wedding guests. Aside from purchasing a guest book cover, couples buy specially designed pages that encourage guests to offer advice, special wishes, and wedding predictions, as well as share their favorite memories of the day. There is even space for guests to draw pictures of the bride and groom!

CENTERPIECES

There's no doubt that a luscious bouquet of fresh flowers can make any table come alive. One can't help but feel a little more joyful at the sight of these amazing gifts of nature. Many of them also produce an intoxicating fragrance.

Brighten Someone Else's Day

If you will use floral bouquets as center-pieces, why not arrange to have someone take the bouquets to a hospital or nursing home once the reception is done?

If you want cut flowers as centerpieces but want to save money, look in the yellow pages for any greenhouses or flower wholesalers in your area. My mom and I were referred to a local greenhouse that carried a wide variety of fresh flowers priced lower than at a florist. Arranging them ourselves—I just wanted loosely arranged garden bouquets—also cut down on costs. Another option is local grocery stores. Many have on-site florists or at least sell inexpensive prearranged bouquets.

Although you can't go wrong with cut flowers, you are not limited to this centerpiece choice. Silk flowers, potted plants, or candles floating in pretty bowls can be just as stunning. For a colorful alternative to flowers, place sugared fruit or lemons and other citrus fruits in glass bowls. A cookie bouquet with enough decorated cookies for each guest can be beautiful and delicious—and it doesn't need a home after the reception.

Another double-duty option is to replace the traditional wedding cake with cake centerpieces for the tables. Check out chapter eight for even more options.

LET THEM EAT CAKE

A beautifully crafted wedding cake captures the attention of guests, especially those with a sweet tooth! Talented cake decorators can turn these edible delights into works of art. Many couples I interviewed noted that their wedding cake was an important feature of the reception.

"Our cake was incredible. We received comments from guests that it was the most beautiful *and* delicious wedding cake they had ever had. . . . It had chocolate "cigarettes" standing on end around each layer and was tied with a red ribbon. Each layer was slightly separated, and there were fresh raspberries between each layer. The inside was yellow cake, chocolate cake, Bailey's [Irish Cream] mousse, and chocolate mousse," says Lynette. She adds that the cake cutting was the highlight of the reception for her and her husband, Charles.

Pat and Chris also received rave reviews about their cake. "After having pictures [taken], we met our guests in the . . . dining room, where they had the most amazing cake. It was quite spectacular, with fondant calla lilies all on a silver platter with real flowers," says Pat.

Linda and Robert said their charm cake was one highlight of their Victorian-themed reception. "We had designed it with a baker but weren't sure how it would turn out. . . . It was better than I ever imagined!" says Linda. The baker baked inside the cake Victorian pull charms, which were taken out after the cake was cut. "All of my bridesmaids pulled a charm telling their fortune," says Linda.

Although many couples perform the traditional cake cutting, the "feeding" portion varied. Some smashed the cake into one another's faces, some simply fed each other, and others, like Darin and me, completely skipped that part.

Some couples didn't even bother with a wedding cake. Some alternatives to the traditional wedding cake include individual cheesecakes, petit fours, and pastries. Susan and Nikhil served their guests special desserts instead of wedding cake. "Instead of a cake, we had a local

CUPCAKE TREE

Looking for an alternative to a wedding cake? What about a cupcake tree? Cupcaketree.com (www.cupcaketree.com) sells cupcake trees that hold between fifty and three hundred cupcakes. When filled with decorated cupcakes, the tree units make for a stunning display.

bakery do individual desserts. [The two of us] still split a small cake, ... but we didn't do it in public. It was more of a private moment of reflection for us," explains Susan.

Nicole and Ned also decided against a traditional wedding cake. "Each person got their own personal chocolate molten cake," says Nicole.

SHOOTING THE RECEPTION

If you want specific moments, people, or even objects at the reception to be captured on film, make sure you let your photographer know. I wish we had more pictures of the tent—both inside and out—and of the various tables. I also would have liked to have had more pictures of Darin and me during the reception, but I didn't think to let the photographer know ahead of time.

If you have friends and family members who enjoy photography, encourage them to take lots of pictures. I had a blast taking black-and-white photos at my friend's wedding, and she was pleased with the outcome. Friends of one couple I interviewed sneaked out during the reception and got their film developed at a one-hour photo lab. The pictures were ready before the event was over.

RECEPTION SHOT LIST

This list includes some traditional and not-so-traditional photo ideas. Be sure to give your photographer a shot list.

- Bride and groom arriving at reception
- Emcee at microphone
- Bride and groom giving speeches
- Bride and groom kissing
- Attendants giving toasts
- Garter toss
- Bouquet toss
- Bride and groom dancing
- Bride and groom cutting the cake
- Bride and groom visiting with guests
- Bride and groom enjoying meal
- People at each table
- Bride laughing
- Groom laughing
- Bride and groom sharing a quiet moment together
- Panoramic shot of reception venue

If you have family or friends who own a digital camera, ask them to use it. That way you'll have computer images to use to make an online wedding page or simply to send to people who couldn't attend the wedding.

You can also provide your guests with disposable cameras, which seems to be fairly popular. FreeWeddingCameras.com (www.freeweddingcameras.com) offers a variety of disposable wedding cameras.

TO TAPE OR NOT TO TAPE

Some couples see a wedding video as a must; others find it unnecessary. Some who want a wedding video, hire a professional; others have a friend or family member run the camera. Although the latter option is cheaper, the outcome might not be ideal.

Either way, it's important to let the videographer know what footage you want and what you don't want. Maybe you want all the toasts on tape but don't care to have a half hour of footage from the dance floor. Maybe you are camera shy and would rather not have the camera pointed at you at all. Don't make the videographer try to read your mind.

Several couples I interviewed had their videographer tape each guest offering congratulations to the bride and groom. What a great way to add a personal touch to the record of your special day!

© 2001 FRANK FROST

A Train Ride Through the Desert

~

SUSAN & NIKHIL

SANTE FE, NEW MEXICO

THE MEETING:	Susan's friend had been trying for years to get Susan to meet Nikhil. Finally, an opportunity presented itself when Nikhil's car broke down while he was vacationing in New Mexico. They fell in love during the week it took to get his car fixed.
THE PROPOSAL:	The couple, having just returned early from a vacation, spent New Year's Eve on the couch nursing colds. Both had been sick before their vacation, but, afraid to ruin one another's trip, kept quiet and went anyway. "I made a comment that each of us should have told the other we were not feeling well—that it was like [the] O. Henry story ["The Gift of the Magi"]. And then I said, 'I guess we should make it official and get married.' And [Nikhil] said, 'You're right. What date do you want?'"
CEREMONY:	A lookout area between Santa Fe and Lamy, New Mexico
RECEPTION:	A cottonwood grove at the Lamy Train Depot and aboard the Santa Fe Southern Railway.
NUMBER OF GUESTS:	50
COST:	$17,900; paid for by the bride and groom and their parents
PLANNING DURATION:	3 months of planning spread over a 6-month period

Susan and Nikhil wanted something different for their wedding. At first they thought about an outdoor wedding at a bed-and-breakfast, a museum, or a garden, but every venue they visited seemed too conventional for their tastes.

Susan says, "We would discuss that we wanted a very fun, casual affair on a Tuesday with good food, good spirits, and good conversation. I would say I wanted to wear purple [and] Nikhil would be in a period costume, and we didn't want an altar. We kept being told, 'You really don't want to do that. It's a wedding—you must have a string quartet, a big cake, a white dress, etc.'" One vendor even told the couple they were "too weird."

In a moment of frustration, Susan suggested to Nikhil that they simply take off on a boat or train and get married. That's when the bells went off, and they remembered the Santa Fe Southern Railway. Susan checked the train's Web site and was elated to discover that the train could be chartered for an entire day. "We went to visit the train, and their response was, 'Ohhh, a wedding. We've done receptions and rehearsal dinners, but never the whole wedding. This could be fun.' That sold us," says Susan.

ALL ABOARD

Susan has always loved trains. In fact, as a child she had a "gigantic" train set and enjoyed spending hours building model train scenes and cars with her dad. What better place for her to get married than on the real thing?

The Santa Fe Southern Railway is a collection of vintage train cars and engines that make pleasure rides through the New Mexico countryside. The couple chose for their wedding a New Jersey commuter car from the 1910 era, a 1940s lounge/observation car, and an open-air car.

The seven-hour journey began at 1:45 P.M., with the couple greeting their guests as they boarded the train. "[That] was our receiving line," says Susan. Fifteen minutes later the train departed from Santa Fe, and guests spread out among the three cars.

Each car had its own appeal. The observation car had a 360-degree view of the New Mexican countryside. The commuter car had seats that swung back so that people could rearrange the way they were facing.

After enjoying beverages and appetizers, the guests exited the train for the half-hour wedding ceremony, which was held outdoors at an overlook on the side of the railroad right-of-way. Following the ceremony, the newlyweds and their guests reboarded the train for a one-hour journey to a depot in Lamy—a small village eighteen miles outside Santa Fe—where a New Mexican buffet dinner awaited them. "We had a tent set up in a cottonwood grove. It was very casual and low key.…We had very simple table settings with white linens and white china," says Susan.

The couple chose to serve just New Mexican food and wine, and they hired a local caterer. "One of our big themes was New Mexico, so we wanted things to be as local as possible," says Susan. They used seven tables and no assigned seating. Dried pansies and lavender, candles, lanterns, and butterfly cutouts served as centerpieces. The couple gave as favors seed packets of New Mexican wildflowers. Some friends later sent them pictures of the flowers growing at their homes.

As a special touch, the couple made a scrapbook with pictures of themselves from birth to their wedding day. The scrapbook, which served as the guest book, also included a picture of each guest. It was circulated at all the prewedding events, including the bridal shower, the "bachelor bonfire," the "anti-bachelorette" party, and the rehearsal dinner, as well as at the wedding itself. "Instead of a list of names we have a wonderful book full of poems, drawings, [and] personal letters," says Susan.

The couple decided against any formal toasts (the maid of honor and best man gave toasts at the rehearsal dinner), although they did steal away for a few moments during the reception to privately toast one another.

They also chose not to have a bouquet toss, a garter toss, or dancing. They didn't even have music. "I don't like loud, distracting music at most weddings—music so loud you can't have a conversation without screaming. We wanted the focus to be on good conversation," says Susan. "Besides, we did have the train whistle!"

FUN SURPRISES

During the dinner stop some special memories were made—and several of them were entirely unplanned. "One of the coolest things was that the train engineer let the guests climb into the engine car and play with the controls," says Susan. Playing hide-and-seek with her nieces and nephews in the old caboose was another highlight.

Then there was the sight of a bridesmaid twirling around in her ball gown. "One of my bridesmaids had always wanted a full ball skirt, so I told her to have one made for her dress. I can still hear her giggles as she kept spinning around so her skirt would move around her," says Susan.

PARTY ON

One more stop at a lookout point on the way back to Santa Fe during sunset was where dessert—not wedding cake—and champagne were served.

By the time the train got moving again it was dark, and Susan says returning to Santa Fe was a highlight. "We were on the open-air car with friends our age, enjoying the stars, and we started passing by people's backyards and crossing major roads. . . . People honked their horns and cheered at us," says Susan.

They pulled into the station at 8:30 P.M.

A WONDERFUL JOURNEY

Susan and Nikhil thought their train ride wedding was as perfect as can be, and so did their guests. Susan says, "The train ride provided the entertainment, so guests just sat back and enjoyed the ride. . . . Our guests loved that they got to spend so much time talking to us, catching up with other friends, and making new friends. As one guest said, 'How often do I get to ride a train for a whole day?'"

Susan and Nikhil's Wedding Budget

Reception venue, food and beverages	$9,800
(including train, dessert and service, tent rental, tables, chairs, linens, glassware, and dishes)	
Attire	$1,200
Flowers	$280
Centerpieces	$30
Photography/videography	$4,000
(amount is for photography only; videography was a gift)	
Stationery	$800
Gifts	$400
Wedding rings	$500
Ceremony	$250
Miscellaneous expenses	$640
(favors, gratuities, marriage license, disposable cameras, photo processing, toasting flutes, flower girl's bucket, ring bearer's box)	
Total	**$17,900**

CHAPTER 6

A Wedding Indoors

Know what's great about indoor weddings? It can be raining cats and dogs outside. The wind can be whipping. A blizzard can descend, or a sleet storm can drop a layer of slush. No matter what the weather is like on your wedding day (yours, of course, will be sunny and gorgeous!), you and your guests will stay comfortable and dry.

A house of worship is probably the most traditional place to host a wedding, but your options aren't limited to the traditional. What about getting married at the bed-and-breakfast you recently visited with your sweetheart? Maybe your aunt's home on the water would be the perfect place to tie the knot. This chapter explores the traditional and the many untraditional places to say "I do."

A CHURCH WEDDING

Many couples feel, for various reasons, a church ceremony is a must. Some brides- and grooms-to-be regularly attend church, so choosing the place of worship in which to say their vows is simple. Other couples only set foot in church on special occasions but feel there is no more sacred a place to say their "I dos." Some couples opt for a church wedding simply for aesthetics: They want a picturesque setting for their wedding. Still others get married in a church because of tradition—like their parents did and their grandparents did.

For Dana and Christopher, who are profiled in chapter three, tradition played a big role when they chose the Little Chapel of the Flowers in Las Vegas. "We chose this location because my parents were married at this chapel more than thirty-five years ago and my grandmother had also gotten married there years ago," says Dana.

Rebecca and Andrew chose their church for not only its beauty but also for its significance to the family. "I was born into [the] church. My grandparents attended this church; my parents attend this church," says Rebecca.

For Darin and me, the decision to get married in a church was affected by tradition but was based overall on practicality. We considered a ceremony outside at our home but realized that would require too much work. We're not churchgoers, but we were both raised with religion—my late grandfather was even a Lutheran minister.

After visiting a few of the beautiful historical churches in our small town, we decided to marry in a small Presbyterian church. The church is charmingly old and has rich wooden pews and stunning stained glass windows—and it is small enough that it worked for the intimacy of our ceremony. The deciding factor, however, was that we found the minister friendly and down to earth.

If you're not affiliated with a church, attend some services at churches in your area. Think about the following questions when you visit:

- Do we feel welcome?

- Can we picture ourselves getting married here?

- Will we feel dwarfed by our surroundings (especially in a large church)?

- Overall, do we have a good feeling about this church?

If you like a church, contact the cleric and get more details (For information on finding an officiant to perform the ceremony, see page 48.)

- Will the church require us to become members or to attend classes or counseling?

- Will the church marry a couple who already lives together?

- Do we have to stick with traditional vows, or can we write our own?

- Are nonbiblical readings or poems permitted during the service?

- Does the church allow photography and videotaping during the service?

- Is an honorarium expected for the use of the church?

- What equipment will the church provide? Can the church's candelabras, candles, speakers, organ, and piano be used?

- Are the aisleways big enough to accommodate a wheelchair?

- Is the church air-conditioned? If not, are fans available in hot weather?

- Does the church have a policy on attire? (Some churches, for example, prefer that a shawl be worn to cover bare shoulders.)

- Is the church's organist available for the ceremony?

- Can we hire our own musician(s) for the service?

- Do musical selections have to meet with the church's approval?

- Are guests allowed to toss rose petals or rice outside after the ceremony?

- Are other ceremonies scheduled on our chosen day? If so, what time(s)?

- Are the church officiant and the organist available for a rehearsal the night before the ceremony?

- Can we put a wreath on the front door?

TWO RELIGIONS; ONE WEDDING

What if a bride- and groom-to-be are of different denominations—e.g., Protestant and Catholic—where should they get married? For some couples this can be a problem.

Kerry and John chose a church that would accommodate both their denominations. "We both wanted a church wedding but didn't want to take sides by having the ceremony in one denomination['s church] or the other. My family is Catholic, and John's is Lutheran, so we searched for a place that would allow us to incorporate parts of each of our traditions as well as provide an uplifting framework into which to place those pieces," says Kerry.

It can be more difficult for some couples to find a compromise, so it's important to tackle this issue early on. (For more on ceremonies, see chapter four, page 57.)

OTHER VENUES FOR AN INDOOR WEDDING

Because you are having a small wedding, you'll have plenty of options for both your ceremony and your reception that many other brides and grooms don't have. A bed-and-breakfast, a small inn, a quaint restaurant, an art museum, a historic mansion—even your own home—are just a few options you will have.

You can choose to have the ceremony and the reception at the same place. Among other things, this can save you money. When you choose one venue for both events, you'll need to decorate only one place and won't need transportation from the ceremony to the reception. You will, however, have to find some way to entertain your guests if you plan to have pictures taken after your ceremony. An earlier cocktail hour might suffice.

No matter what you decide, start calling as soon as possible to check availability of the various venues that pique your interest.

If a venue provides food, ask them to send you a menu along with prices. Although the menu selections sound tantalizing, make sure you try the food first! (This is a great excuse for a night out with your honey.) Some venues even offer complimentary sample meals.

Another thing you will need to decide is if you want cocktail service, a seated meal, buffet or food stations, and you'll need to find out if you can bring your own alcohol.

KEEPING COOL

If you are planning a summer wedding inside a church that does not have air-conditioning, try to have a morning ceremony. Make sure you set up several fans inside the church, and find out if the church windows can be opened. Provide a cooler full of bottled water at the entrance, if this is permitted. Consider handing out paper fans to guests.

QUESTIONS TO ASK WHEN CHOOSING A VENUE:

- ❧ Is smoking allowed?

- ❧ Are there noise restrictions? (A bed-and-breakfast, for instance, might not let you hire an eight-piece rock band for the occasion.)

- ❧ Is there a dance floor? If not, is there enough room for people to dance?

- ❧ Will the place be exclusively ours for the day, or will others be in the vicinity? (If you choose an inn, for example, other inn guests might be present.)

- ❧ Is there ample parking?

- ❧ Are there time restrictions? (If you book a place until midnight, partying until 2 A.M. might not be an option.)

- ❧ Is the place wheelchair accessible?

- ❧ Can we decorate the place the way we like?

- ❧ Will we have access to the site early enough to decorate?

- ❧ Is the place air-conditioned?

- ❧ What are the bathrooms like?

- ❧ Is there a place we can set up a microphone and speakers for the emcee?

- ❧ What's the lighting like? (Bright artificial lighting doesn't make for a very romantic setting.)

- ❧ Are children allowed?

BED-AND-BREAKFAST OR INN WEDDINGS

Bed-and-breakfasts and inns (the terms are often interchangeable) can be ideal for small weddings. They can offer a unique and intimate atmosphere—and maybe even overnight package deals for you and your wedding party.

You might know of one with special meaning to you because you and your sweetie found it while traveling or because it's near your home. If not, check the numerous guidebooks and Internet sites that give details on—including amenities, pricing, and ratings—bed-and-breakfasts and inns throughout North America and the rest of the world. BedandBreakfast.com (www.bedandbreakfast.com) lists more than 27,000 bed-and-breakfasts throughout the world, while www.bbonline.com has details on more than 4,500 bed-and-breakfasts—and it has plenty of pictures! CharmingCountryInns.com (www.charmingcountryinns.com) lists hundreds of little-known, out-of-the-way inns and bed-and-breakfasts throughout North America.

"I Do" at a Historic Missouri Bed-and-Breakfast

THERESE AND MARK chose for their wedding the Inn St. Gemme Beauvais, a bed-and-breakfast in Ste. Genevieve, Missouri, ninety minutes from their Missouri home. "We chose it after we spent a week there on vacation. It was such a lovely, peaceful place—far away from the hectic day-to-day [routine] of our lives," says Therese.

The inn, which was built in 1848 as a private residence, is the oldest bed-and-breakfast in Missouri. Although it has many modern amenities, the three-story Greek Revival brick mansion retains the charm of the era in which it was built.

The couple and their thirty guests enjoyed an early-evening outdoor ceremony on the grounds of the inn, followed by a sit-down dinner reception in the inn's dining room. "We didn't spend a lot of money to decorate the dining room. …The inn provided cloth tablecloths, napkins, silverware, tableware, candles, and fresh flowers," says Therese.

The dining room provided a cozy atmosphere for the celebration. "The lighting was low, and since everyone was so close together it was a very intimate, 'homey' feeling," she says.

Since dancing wasn't possible in the small dining area, the couple arranged to have their first dance under the gazebo in the garden after the meal. The couple then headed to their room, while their guests continued to enjoy the surroundings. "Everyone thought they had seen the last of us, but we changed our clothes and came [back] out to mingle a bit. … I was walking around barefoot, in shorts and a T-shirt, with my veil and tiara on," says Therese.

Aside from a few minor glitches, the $8,000 event was everything the bride and groom had expected. "I liked the fact that we were able to have the entire place to ourselves for the weekend. Also, it was wonderful to be able to spend the night before the wedding at the inn. We were able to get a lot of things done the day before instead of waiting until the morning of. It helped create a much more relaxed environment," Therese says.

HISTORICAL BUILDINGS

You don't have to be a history buff to appreciate the beauty of old buildings. Whether the architecture dates back to the Victorian period or the era of Art Deco, historical buildings retain a sentimental charm that modern buildings simply don't have.

Because historical buildings are such unique structures, they can add character to your wedding and interest to your wedding photographs. They can provide for both your ceremony and your reception a backdrop that is far from ordinary.

To find such a building for your wedding, visit historical sites, including museums, in your desired location. Not all historical structures are available for weddings, so if you've fallen in love with a building, make sure you find out well in advance whether or not weddings can be hosted there. Some might open their grounds but not the inside to you. Others might allow a ceremony but not food and beverages.

A Renaissance Wedding in a Historic Building

TERRY AND SHANNON chose a building from the late 1920s in Tecumseh, Kansas, for their Renaissance-themed wedding. The stone and brick building called A Place in Time once served as the local community building but now operates as a learning institute as well as a wedding venue.

Terry and Shannon held their ceremony in a large room on the main floor. "The room was lit with icicle lights. They looked like stars at dusk," says Terry.

Instead of a traditional ceremony, the couple had a judge perform a Christian medieval ceremony. In keeping with the theme, the couple hired a trio to play Renaissance-style music on dulcimers and guitars. After the ten-minute ceremony, the forty-five guests went downstairs for a luncheon reception. "It was decorated like a French castle courtyard, with vines, arches, and ponds," says Terry.

The owners of the venue catered everything except the punch and the wedding cake. "We had [a] simple fare of baked rolls, meats and cheeses, fresh fruits and veggies, punch, coffees and teas, and, of course, the cake," says Terry. The owners also took care of many other wedding-related details. "They did all the setup . . . —centerpieces, decorations, coordinating, rehearsal, cleanup—and they took care of the gifts [and] cards. Anything we needed, [the owner] was there as the wedding coordinator," says Terry.

The couple says having their wedding at A Place in Time kept their costs down (their wedding cost $3,000) and made for less stress because of the all-inclusive service.

ART GALLERIES

Are you an art lover? If so, you might celebrate your nuptials amongst one-of-a-kind works of art. Brides and grooms who want art to be part of their special day can check out one of many U.S. art galleries that host weddings.

To find an art gallery that suits you, visit galleries in your area or galleries in your chosen wedding location. Ask if they are available for weddings, find out what exhibits are planned for the date of your wedding (an exhibit of pornography throughout the ages can rule out a gallery), and find out if the available space is in the gallery area or in an artless side room.

You could include a guided tour for your guests as part of the wedding day festivities. This could be the perfect way for them to pass the time when you and your honey are getting your pictures taken.

An Artful Reception

ELIZABETH AND CHRISTIAN chose to have their December wedding at an arts center in Tolland, Connecticut. The couple, who spent $11,000 on their wedding, wanted a reception venue that was cozy, intimate, elegant, and affordable.

Neither of them had been to the Arts Center of Tolland before, and both were amazed by the building's beauty. Aside from the exquisite architecture, which included huge windows, wood floors, and an original tin ceiling, the place was full of art. "Work from local artists was hung throughout the building. Many of the pieces depicted landscape scenes of the towns we grew up in," says Elizabeth.

According to Elizabeth, guests enjoyed viewing the artwork before and after dinner. "I was told that before we arrived the guests were mingling and looking at the art while the hors d'oeuvres were passed and the pianist played. I noticed that after the deejay ended some guests viewed the pieces, too," she says. "A few guests were even inquiring about purchasing some pieces."

The couple made their surroundings even more beautiful by decorating the venue in a Christmas theme. Busy as little elves, the couple and some relatives and friends set up a Christmas tree in the corner of the reception room. They decorated the tree with doves, lights, pearl strands, and glass balls. They also used garland, swags, and wreaths to make the place look festive. "Except catering and flowers, we did everything ourselves. I believe that is one of the reasons my wedding is so very special to me. I knew exactly the amount of effort that went into everything," she says.

Elizabeth says the arts center was a great bargain and made for a perfect atmosphere for the wedding reception.

RESTAURANTS

Picture a wedding in a quaint bistro in your neighborhood or at a chic downtown restaurant with a stunning view of the city skyline. Restaurants can be wonderful venues for small weddings and were quite popular with the couples I interviewed. Although all restaurants are different, most have intimate surroundings—and offer plenty of convenience. Having a restaurant reception means not having to rent chairs, tables, and tabletop stuff—including the food. No need to hire a caterer when the chef is in the house.

You can go as formal or informal as you like when choosing a restaurant. If you're crazy about Mexican food, have your reception at your favorite Mexican restaurant. If sophisticated is what you want, check out the top fine-dining haunts in your wedding city.

Jennifer and Mark chose La Fogata, an upscale Mexican restaurant in San Antonio, Texas, because they wanted a reception with the Mexican feel of their ceremony location—a historic mission in San Antonio. The couple rented a semiprivate area in the restaurant and had plenty of privacy for their celebratory meal.

After their church ceremony, Danielle and Shawn had a reception at Schuler's Restaurant & Pub in Marshall, Michigan. "It was where my parents-in-law went after their wedding, so it had a bit of sentimental value," says Danielle. Danielle and Shawn and twenty-one guests enjoyed a sit-down meal in a private room in the restaurant. The couple paid for the wedding themselves and cut expenses by having no music. "We didn't have dancing, so I was a little worried that people wouldn't have as much fun, but it ended up being fine," says Danielle.

Ebony and Jorge had forty people at their reception at Villa Barone Ristorante, a Bronx, New York, restaurant that specializes in Italian cuisine. Unlike Jennifer and Mark and Danielle and Shawn, this couple had many traditional wedding reception elements, including dancing. Holding a small reception at a restaurant helped to make the event more affordable for the couple.

A Throwback to the Forties

KRISTEN AND STEPHEN stepped inside the Granite Room in New York City's City Hall Restaurant and were instantly dazzled. The underground room is incredible in detail and very dramatic, with cast-iron columns, a massive walnut and brick bar, arched brick and granite ceilings, and granite walls. "It has a speakeasy/supper club feel," says Kristen.

Kristen, who designs restaurant kitchens for a living, says both she and her husband are "foodies" and felt there was no better place than the restaurant to have their reception.

In keeping with the look of the restaurant, the couple incorporated other elements from the 1940s—including a six-piece swing band. Kristen also made some period fashion statements. "My vintage jewelry and handbag were from the era, and the style of my hair also came from the era," she says.

Guests devoured hors d'oeuvres and a large seafood tower during the cocktail hour, held in the same room as the reception. "[This] actually made it more intimate because [everyone] really got to know the room [and other guests] instead of getting shuffled around," says Kristen.

For dinner, guests chose from menu selections the couple had specified for the occasion. "Having a small wedding in a restaurant gave us the ability to offer our guests steak or lamb chops cooked to their individual liking. Trying to do this with a larger party or at a [reception] hall would not have worked out as well," says Kristen.

LODGES

Lodges come in all shapes, sizes, and styles. Some are basic, offering a casual setting. Others are sophisticated and elegant. No matter the style, a lodge can make for a cozy spot for a wedding. Since many are off the beaten path and near lakes, forests, or mountains, they can offer lovely, picturesque surroundings for your nuptials.

If you want the rustic beauty a lodge has to offer and already have one in mind—

maybe the one your family has visited every year since you were a tot—you're ahead of the game. If you're still searching for one, ask friends and relatives if they recommend any particular lodges. Make sure you get plenty of information, including pictures, for each lodge. Magazines on outdoor life are another resource, as are travel bureaus in your wedding locale. For online research, simply type into your favorite search engine your chosen location along with "lodge." Remember to call and ask if the lodges accommodate weddings.

A Lodge Wedding in the Rocky Mountains

CARI AND JEREMY from Houston, Texas, both love the mountains, especially in the winter. So, what better place to get married than the foothills of the Rocky Mountains?

The couple picked January as their month to wed and the historic Chief Hosa Lodge in Golden, Colorado, as the location. Chief Hosa Lodge is a historical landmark designed and built with hand-quarried Colorado rainbow granite in 1916 by famous architect J.J. Benedict. The lodge, located inside Denver's twenty-four hundred acre Genesee Mountain Park, offers breathtaking views of the Continental Divide. Wildlife, including herds of elk and buffalo, grazes in the park.

Cari and Jeremy had a traditional Christian ceremony, complete with a string quartet, attended by sixty-five guests in a small stone chapel on the lodge premises. "We had candelabras at the front, and each guest had a candle as well. White lights were also strung across the wood beams in the chapel," says Cari.

The reception was held inside the lodge in a stone room that has vaulted ceilings and two fireplaces. A skylight in the room provided a perfect view of the full moon. Cari and Jeremy decorated the room in a winter-wonderland theme using silver and white. Aside from its beauty, the historic lodge is known for its award-winning cuisine, which Cari and Jeremy say lived up to its reputation. After dinner, the couple surprised their guests by heating up the dance floor. "Jeremy and I took dance lessons for six months prior to our wedding and surprised our family and friends with our expert fox-trot," says Cari.

For the send-off, guests lit sparklers and lined the walkway leaving the lodge, and the couple dashed to their getaway car. Cari says she wouldn't have changed a thing about their $17,000 wedding. "We talked and danced with all the guests and truly had fun at our wedding!"

AT-HOME WEDDINGS

Can there be a more intimate setting for a wedding than someone's home? The living room of a home can provide a perfect backdrop for an intimate ceremony. For the reception, a home's dining room or kitchen can be ideal.

If you want an at-home wedding, you have "intimate" covered, but you have a few other things to consider. The first is space: Can the home accommodate your guests without making them feel claustrophobic? The next is work: Are you—and the homeowner, if the home is not yours—up for the work involved in preparing for an at-home wedding? Cleaning and decorating the home can be major chores.

Third is facilities: Does the home have enough bathrooms to accommodate your guests, and can the bathrooms take the overtime? Last, but not least, is the homeowner's piece of mind: Is having your guests traipse through the home tolerable?

A Simple At-Home Wedding in Ohio

JULIE AND MIKE felt they had better things to spend their money on than a large, lavish wedding, so they opted for a simple wedding. Time was another factor in their decision to have a wedding with only eight guests: Julie and Mike met only three weeks prior to their nuptials. "I just knew we could be good together," says Julie. "I was at the point where I knew myself well enough to know he was right for me."

Julie felt that her childhood home —Julie's mother still lived there, but her father had passed away—was the ideal spot for the ceremony. Julie says preparing the brick ranch home for the event was simple. Cleaning the house was all that was involved, since the couple had no special wedding decorations. "The only special thing my mom did was place a [photo] of my late father on the sideboard, where it would be in plain view. I remember her saying something like, 'This way James can watch too.'"

The couple didn't even send out invitations for the wedding, they simply invited people by phone. The mayor of the town performed the ceremony in the home's kitchen. There was no special aisle or altar. "The kitchen table had been moved out of the way to allow everyone to stand more closely together," says Julie. There wasn't even wedding music. "I actually think that added to the intimacy. It was sort of a hushed atmosphere. Quiet and serene," says Julie.

Even though her father couldn't be there, Julie says that having the ceremony in that home made her feel connected to him. "I had lived my entire life there until I was twenty-one. . . . My dad was the original owner of the house, and I remember how proud he was when he made the last house payment. To be married there made me feel closer to my dad. . . . It just felt right," says Julie.

OTHER INDOOR LOCATIONS

This chapter has covered just a few possibilities for an indoor wedding. You have many more options, including country clubs, breweries, wineries, banquet halls, and skyscrapers—to name a few. Don't be afraid to explore more-unusual locations, as well. Some extraordinary locations are detailed below:

- **Jules' Undersea Lodge** in Key Largo, Florida, is an underwater hotel that offers couples the chance to tie the knot five fathoms below the sea. This unusual venue has a wet-room entrance area, two bedrooms, and a common room encompassing the living space, dining area, and kitchen. The wedding couple has to scuba dive to get to the hotel, where they are welcomed with romantic music and fresh flowers. Couples who get married here have exclusive use of the hotel during their stay. A notary public dives down to the hotel and performs the ceremony, usually at 3 P.M. After the toasts are made, the hotel "mer-chef" scuba dives to the hotel to prepare a meal for the couple.

- If you'd rather say your vows in the air, why not get married in a helicopter, high above the Las Vegas strip at night? **Maverick Helicopter Tours** offers wedding packages for couples looking for some adventurous, midflight "I dos." One helicopter accommodates the bride and groom, the officiant, and up to three guests (more seats can be purchased for an extra fee). The limo ride to and from your hotel, the officiant fee, the flowers, the cake, and a picnic are included in the package.

- If you're a stargazer, the **Christa McAuliffe Planetarium** in Concord, New Hampshire, might be the perfect venue for your event. Couples can rent the entire planetarium for a night and take their guests on an astronomical adventure with a planetarium show followed by a meal. Private receptions at the planetarium have ranged from hors d'oeuvres only to full sit-down dinners. For an extra fee, the museum will offer your guests educational demonstrations or telescopes.

- Do you love to shop? Do you love it enough to make it part of your nuptials? If so, you might get married at the **Mall of America** in Bloomington, Minnesota. This seventy-eight acre, four-level complex is home to the Chapel of Love, an indoor garden wedding chapel that has hosted thousands of weddings.

- If you crave something really unusual and don't mind braving the cold, consider the **Ice Hotel Quebec-Canada**. This structure is built entirely from ice and snow. Within it are numerous bedrooms, a cinema, a chapel, a reception room, a bar, functional fireplaces, and hot tubs. The hotel offers a wedding package for two. The package includes a civil ceremony in the pristine ice chapel, one bottle of champagne, two ice-sculpted champagne goblets, and a wedding planner to assist with the arrangements. Other wedding-related services, such as transportation, photography, and entertainment, can be arranged by the hotel. The package includes access to the hotel for up to eight people including the bride and groom.

If you want to stay in the U.S., check out the **Aurora Ice Hotel** at Chena Hot Springs Resort near Fairbanks, Alaska. The Aurora is the first ice hotel built in the U.S.

DRESSING FOR YOUR INTIMATE INDOOR WEDDING

The garb: For some couples it's the top priority; for others, it's just another item on the wedding checklist. Regardless of your perspective, there are a few things to keep in mind before you start shopping for duds.

EIGHT INFLUENCES ON WHAT YOU WEAR

§1§ **Budget:** How much do you want to spend on your attire? Generally, wedding planners say you should allot about 11 percent of your budget for attire, but not everyone follows this estimate. Plenty of brides have found wedding dresses off the rack at department stores or online at eBay (www.ebay.com) for less than two hundred bucks. (See page 35 for more information on saving money on attire.)

§2§ **Style:** What type of wedding are you planning? For a formal church wedding, an elegant full-length satin bridal gown—complete with sequins and a train—and a tuxedo with tails might be appropriate. However, for a casual candlelit ceremony at a bed-and-breakfast, a more simple bride's dress and khakis paired with a white dress shirt might be better.

§3§ **Self-Expression:** Who says brides have to wear white? If you're the unconventional type, you might choose clothing that expresses your free spirit—maybe a red dress, a lush purple velvet gown, or a sundress. Grooms can be a bit daring, too—perhaps with a pink shirt or a funky tie.

§4§ **Shape:** As you probably know, wedding dresses come in several styles and with varying necklines (see www.weddingplans.com.cy/accessories.htm for a description of the various types). Let your body type help determine the style of dress you choose. For instance, a bride with a fuller figure probably should avoid a

did *YOU* *know?*

The average bride will try on twelve wedding dresses.

(source: Brandweek*)*

sheath. A petite bride probably should choose a dress that doesn't have lots of volume. No matter what your body type, the key to success is to try on many different styles.

⸭5⸭ Time Frame: If your wedding attire is important to you, start shopping early. Give yourself a chance to try on lots of clothes. If you have to order a wedding dress or tuxedo, you won't be in a time crunch.

⸭6⸭ Place: The most obvious place to shop for a wedding dress is at a local bridal store. A more adventurous option is to shop online. Here are just a few sites to check out: www.alfredsungbridals.com, www.ebay.com, www.davidsbridal.com, www.thebridalworld.com, www.weddingexpressions.com, and www.houseof brides.com.

⸭7⸭ Accessories: Accessories can be a downright crucial component to your wedding ensemble. If you are looking for variety—or you just want to save money—try shopping online. Here are a couple sites to check out: www.bridal headpieces.com and www.weddingexpressions.com.

⸭8⸭ Attendants: Thankfully, couples now have plenty of options these days when it comes to dressing their attendants. Gone are the days when it was absolutely necessary for the bridesmaids to wear identical dresses and matching dyed shoes. Now, the rules are more flexible. You can have the bridemaids do the following:

- wear identical dresses

- wear dresses in the same color and fabric, but let each bridesmaid choose the style of dress that suits her best

- wear dresses in the same color, but in the fabrics and styles they individually choose

- wear whatever they want—they will love you more than they already do

did *you* ?
know !

Attire wasn't a huge issue for Darin and me, and it turned out to be a simple, stress-free wedding detail. Thankfully, I found my dress quickly, and we settled on Darin's and his best man's tuxes early. At my request, my maid of honor picked her own dress based on the color that I preferred. To outfit my nieces—the flower girl and the ring bearer—I told their mother what color I wanted, and she had the dresses made in styles that suited the girls. It made for a simple, stress-free arrangement.

© 2002 TAINA CRUZADO COTE

A Brunch Reception at a Historic Inn

~

HEATHER & ANTHONY

ROCKPORT, MASSACHUSETTS

THE MEETING:	The couple met while listening to a mutual friend's jazz band play at a local coffeehouse. "We were introduced and played Monopoly while listening to the band. Our first date was four days later," says Heather.
THE PROPOSAL:	During a weekend vacation in Rockport, Anthony suggested a walk on the beach. "By the time we got to the beach, the sky was thunderstorm black and the waves were picking up," says Heather. With thunder and lightning as their backdrop, Anthony got down on one knee and proposed. "I said yes, totally surprised," says Heather.
CEREMONY & RECEPTION:	Emerson Inn by the Sea, Rockport, Massachusetts
NUMBER OF GUESTS:	67
COST:	$17,200; paid for by the bride and groom with some help from the bride's parents
PLANNING DURATION:	16 months

Heather and Anthony live in New Haven, Connecticut, but they decided to tie the knot in Rockport, Massachusetts, because the seaside town has special meaning to them. "My family has a second home there. It's also where we got engaged, and we love it there!" says Heather.

The couple decided early on to keep their guest list small. Aside from the intimate appeal of a small wedding, having fewer guests meant the couple could splurge. "If we [had] had a large wedding, we couldn't have had it at the Emerson, where the food is absolutely fantastic," says Heather.

The Emerson Inn by the Sea, located an hour north of Boston on the Atlantic Ocean, is a traditional inn built in 1846. "We had never stayed at the Emerson before, but it is one of the famous historic inns [in the area], and I'd seen it before and knew it was beautiful," says Heather. The Emerson Inn by the Sea also allowed them to have a wedding near the water.

According to the couple, the inn provided them with "one-stop shopping." The venue accommodated their ceremony and reception, as well as providing overnight lodging for them and some of their guests. The venue also provided a wedding coordinator. "She answered all our questions and really made the whole planning and wedding day go very smoothly," says Heather.

THE "I DOS"

The couple originally planned to have their ceremony on the inn grounds, but a cold snap led the couple to say their "I dos" in the inn's grand parlor. The parlor has wide-plank wood floors, large picture windows, and high ceilings. Period furniture, Oriental rugs, and artwork adorn the room, while a large staircase enters into the middle of it.

Before the ceremony, the wedding guests formed a circle around the staircase. One by one, the honor attendants descended the staircase, followed by the bride's parents and finally the bride. Meantime, the groom, along with the justice of the peace, waited patiently on the landing of the staircase, where the vows took place. "We wrote our own vows. That makes the ceremony itself much more real. When you have to decide what you promise to another person for the rest of your life, it becomes almost a meditation," says Heather.

According to Heather, she and Anthony are both inspired by Tibetan monastic art and Buddhism. They used deep crimson, burgundy, and gold—colors commonly found in Buddhist temples—for their decor and the Buddhist Knot of Eternity on their stationery. Buddhism also inspired the favors: antique brass bells. "They are used to signal endings and beginnings," says Heather.

THE BRUNCH CELEBRATION

In the grand parlor, a cocktail hour and brunch buffet, which included omelettes, French toast, pancakes, bacon, sausage, seafood, and a carving station with roast beef and turkey, followed the ceremony.

Instead of assigning seats, the couple let guests choose where they wanted to sit. "We had the bridal party and those in the wedding ceremony at one table. Everyone else was where they wanted to be," says Heather.

Because Rockport is a dry town and the bride and groom aren't big drinkers, the only alcohol served was sparkling wine. (The couple had to hire a bartender and supply the alcohol.) "Our wedding was …early enough in the day [that] people had the evening to go to Gloucester [a nearby town] and have drinks if they pleased," says Heather

A pianist played retro jazz tunes on the grand piano in the parlor while guests enjoyed brunch. "There was no bouquet toss, garter toss, first dance, announcing of 'Mr. & Mrs.' (especially since I didn't change my name), electric slide, or bunny hop—none of that, thank goodness," Heather says.

Heather describes the overall atmosphere as "celebratory, relaxed, calm, fun, and happy." She says, "Having a celebration at such a beautiful place made everyone feel good. People feel special in a special place, and the combination of the inn, the water, and the people made it completely and uniquely special."

Their guests also gave the wedding rave reviews. "We thought people would say nice things, but we didn't expect the outpouring we got. We had comments like 'That was the most elegant wedding I've ever been to' and 'It was a perfect day!'" Heather says. One comment, however, stood out above all the rest. "I think the best compliment anyone gave us was 'Your wedding was uniquely you,'" says Heather.

Heather points out that one of the biggest benefits of having a wedding at a historic inn or bed-and-breakfast is that you can always go back and relive your wedding-day memories. "For the rest of our lives we can spend weekends at the place we had our wedding," says Heather. "We're already planning our first anniversary there …and the second and the third.…"

Heather and Anthony's Wedding Budget

Reception venue, music, food, and beverages (including cake and service)	$7,930
Attire	$1,980
Flowers	$920
Photography	$4,700
Stationery (given to the couple as a gift)	$0
Gifts	$580
Wedding rings	$820
Ceremony (the justice of the peace was forty-five minutes late, so the $100 fee was waived)	$0
Miscellaneous expenses (favors and centerpieces)	$270
Total	**$17,200**

CHAPTER 7

Saying "I Do" Outdoors

Imagine a garden in full kaleidoscopic bloom, or picture a sprawling landscape shaded by tall trees and fragrant flowering shrubs. Imagine the soft scents of lavender, roses, and peonies. Imagine a sweetly singing cardinal and chirping chickadees. Then imagine being surrounded by nature's divine splendor as you are pronounced husband and wife.

Not surprisingly, more and more couples are using nature as a wedding backdrop. Whether your celebration will be held in a garden, vineyard, forest, or park; aboard a yacht; or on the grounds of your favorite bed-and-breakfast, the setting will be spectacular. You must, however, consider many things when you are at the mercy of Mother Nature.

IS AN OUTDOOR WEDDING RIGHT FOR YOU?

Having an outdoor wedding isn't for every couple. There are several topics to consider. To start, think about the questions below:

- Are you a worrywart? If so, you might want to skip the idea of marrying outdoors. If the outdoors is a must, have a solid backup plan. Wedding planning can be stressful enough without the added fret over a possible downpour on your wedding day.

- Do you constantly need to be in control? If your answer is yes, planning an outdoor wedding might cause you some serious headaches. After all, there's no controlling the elements.

- Will the weather determine whether or not you view your wedding day as a success? Does the idea of celebrating your nuptials under gray skies and raindrops make you shudder? If so, plan an indoor wedding or an outdoor one with a solid backup plan.

- Do you have allergies? If so, the outdoors might give you a red runny nose and itchy eyes on your wedding day. You could also end up sneezing between—or during—toasts.

If you decide an outdoor wedding is for you, read on. You'll see exactly what to do to start planning your big day!

A Vineyard Wedding Planned From the Heart

MISTY AND MICHAEL, from Los Angeles, California, chose for their wedding site a winery on California's central coast. The couple had visited the region before and fallen in love with the area. They chose Castoro Cellars because of its warmth and natural beauty, according to Misty.

Because the winery was a five-hour drive for the majority of their guests, Misty and Michael had made hotel arrangements for many of them. The couple also chartered a bus to pick up their guests from the hotel and transport them to and from the winery.

A small stone circle amidst the trees and grass in the vineyard was the evening ceremony's setting. With the guests forming a circle around the couple, Misty and Michael said their vows—which Misty, a writer, had written. "All of our guests could hear every word of the ceremony without any microphones. They could hear our vows, our promises. Some could even hear our whispers," says Misty. "And we could hear the sniffles and even the sighs of our mothers."

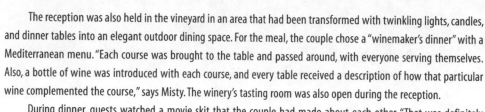

The reception was also held in the vineyard in an area that had been transformed with twinkling lights, candles, and dinner tables into an elegant outdoor dining space. For the meal, the couple chose a "winemaker's dinner" with a Mediterranean menu. "Each course was brought to the table and passed around, with everyone serving themselves. Also, a bottle of wine was introduced with each course, and every table received a description of how that particular wine complemented the course," says Misty. The winery's tasting room was also open during the reception.

During dinner, guests watched a movie skit that the couple had made about each other. "That was definitely everyone's favorite moment!" says Misty. Speeches and dancing followed the meal, along with a live New Orleans jazz band performing the songs of Ella Fitzgerald and Billie Holiday. "The reception was beautiful, fun, lively, loving, warm, and just 'wow.' I mean, we planned the darn thing, and we were impressed!" says Misty.

The total cost of their sixty-guest wedding, which the bride and groom paid for themselves, was $18,000.

MORE PLANNING—AND MORE MONEY

When planning my outdoor reception, one of my first thoughts was: "It'll be small, so it won't require that much work to plan." Was I wrong! I have no doubt that I put just as much effort into planning our fifty-guest wedding as I would have for a wedding with a guest list of two hundred!

An outdoor wedding oftentimes requires more planning than an indoor wedding does—and it can cost more money. If you have an outdoor ceremony, chances are you will have to rent chairs and a tent. If you don't want to bother with a tent, do have an indoor backup plan in case of inclement weather.

Unless you are getting married at an outdoor facility that provides all the nitty-gritty for your reception, you will need to provide or rent tables, linens, glassware, and dinnerware. If you plan to feed your guests, you need to hire a caterer or sweet-talk family into preparing the food, and you need to hire servers unless you will have a buffet. Hiring a bartender is necessary if you will serve drinks. On top of all that, you need to consider how to run electricity to your tent, what type of rest room facilities to have, and whether to have a dance floor.

GO WITH THE FLOW

Flexibility is important when planning an outdoor wedding. You might have strong ideas of what you want: Write them down, but keep in mind that your list of ideals might have to be altered. Keep a strong vision of what you want, but also stay open to other possibilities.

USE PROTECTION

If you are planning an outdoor wedding, use protection against the elements. Don't become another horror story of a daring couple whose decision to marry left them and their guests all wet.

Rain is not your only weather concern. A hot sun blazing down on you and your guests will at the very least cause discomfort; for some people, it can cause sunburn and heatstroke. That can make memories your guests won't appreciate. If you're a risk taker and don't want to bother with a tent, make some sort of backup plan for inclement weather.

OUTDOOR STYLES

Anything goes for outdoor weddings, and the styles are limitless. Some couples opt for champagne brunches, afternoon parties, or cocktail receptions instead of formal dinner receptions. Couples who want a laid-back wedding can have, for example, a casual lobster bake on the beach where guests wear shorts and sandals and dance to the sounds of a reggae band. Playful types—especially those who invite lots of children—can create a carnival-like atmosphere with games, clowns, cotton candy, balloons, and streamers.

OUTDOOR WEDDING CHECKLIST

Below is a general checklist of items you may have to rent or provide for depending on the location of your outdoor wedding:

- Tent
- Chairs
- Chair covers
- Tables
- Linens
- Dinnerware
- Glassware
- Fly tents for appetizers, desserts, wedding cake
- Electrical outlets
- Microphone
- Stage
- Rest room facilities
- Dance floor
- Tent lighting and decorations
- Bug spray

Outdoor weddings can still be sophisticated. The right flooring, lighting, and decor can transform an ordinary tent into an elegant outdoor ballroom—perfect for a cocktail or dinner reception.

WHERE TO HAVE YOUR OUTDOOR WEDDING

Perhaps you know you want an outdoor wedding. Now the question is where to hold it. The possibilities are boundless, but just loving a place does not make it suitable for a wedding.

One must for an outdoor wedding is some form of shelter, such as a tent or nearby building. If you choose to have the reception outdoors, the location also should meet the following criteria:

No Surprises

So that the guests can dress appropriately, make sure they know you're having an outdoor event. You don't want Grandma to show up in four-inch stilettos at a garden wedding!

- not get muddy or flooded if it rains.

- allow for electricity if you plan to have lights and/or a sound system.

- provide or allow access to a stove, a refrigerator, and table space if you plan to serve a meal.

- offer parking that is close by—it's a wedding, not a hike (unless you want a hiking wedding).

- have rest rooms or space for portable toilets.

BEACHES

Beaches can be perfect for weddings, and they span the globe. In addition to an abundance of location choices, beach weddings mean some extra planning concerns. Remember that the weather can be unpredictable and that the wind can really pick up over the water. Have some form of shelter *and* a backup plan. Provide umbrellas and sunscreen for your guests so they don't get scorched. Consider having a more casual affair, so that sand is less likely to clash with your guests' attire. (See page 132 for beach theme ideas.)

GARDENS

With their flowers and lush greenery, gardens can provide a stunning backdrop for a wedding. An afternoon wedding in the garden, with cocktails and appetizers, can be a wonderful way to celebrate your big day. A sit-down meal in the evening can also be marvelous—but don't forget the citronella candles and the bug spray! (See page 132 for garden theme ideas.)

FORESTS

Being surrounded by tall trees can give a wedding a truly intimate atmosphere. Imagine an autumn wedding held in a forest of crimson sugar maples. Not only would it be beautiful, but imagine all those intoxicating autumn scents! Forest weddings can be enchanting, but remember, bugs can be a problem. If you plan on tying the knot in the woods, be prepared!

VINEYARDS

You don't have to be a wine lover to appreciate the beauty of a vineyard. Because they offer picturesque settings as well as places to indulge guests in wine tastings and tours, vineyards have become popular spots for weddings. Many couples who choose a vineyard venue incorporate the wine theme into their nuptials by serving fine wine and using colors, decor, and favors that fit the theme.

PARKS

Many parks—ranging from historical sites to woodlands—permit weddings. While some parks have strict rules about weddings (e.g., ceremonies only, no alcohol, no chairs or tables), others have fewer regulations. If you think a park in your area would be perfect for your wedding, make sure you find out what restrictions apply. National parks are also popular for outdoor weddings. Ellen and Tony (see page 172), for instance, got married at Yosemite National Park. The couple had their ceremony in a small amphitheater in the park and their reception in a shaded picnic area in Yosemite Valley.

WEIRD, WACKY, OR A BIT BIZARRE

Couples who like to do things a bit differently can choose from a slew of outdoor possibilities. Thrill seekers might consider an outdoor adventure wedding. This could be a ceremony in the Grand Canyon, on a roller coaster, or in the wilderness in wintertime. The truly daring might consider bungee jumping into their nuptials.

If you go with an adventure wedding, don't count on much participation from your friends and family. You also might have a difficult time finding an officiant. That said,

GARDEN SHOWERS

Do you and your mate love to garden? If so, why not have a couples shower with a garden theme. Ask the host(s) to request that guests bring gifts you can use outdoors. The invitations and food can also tie in with the garden theme.

several companies do offer "extreme" wedding packages. Rabbi Jamie Korngold (see www.adventurerabbi.com) will marry couples on ski trips, rafting adventures, climbing trips, or wilderness hikes.

Want to get married on the top of an Alaskan glacier? Check out www.pearson spond.com. What about tying the knot on horseback or inside a candlelit cave? Go to www.spiritualweddings.com. If an African safari is more your style, check out www.afroventures.com. There's even a company that will arrange weddings on a volcano (see www.maui.net/~anointed).

Not looking for a wedding-day thrill but still want a place that is unique? Several unusual locations throughout the U.S. accommodate weddings.

- For those who adore the writing of Edgar Allan Poe, there's the **Edgar Allan Poe Museum** in Richmond, Virginia. The museum is home to the Poe house, the oldest house in Richmond and a place Edgar Allan Poe visited. Wedding ceremonies are held in the Enchanted Garden, which is modeled after Poe's poem "To One in Paradise."

- Want a sea lion for a ring bearer? If you tie the knot at **SeaWorld Orlando** you can make animals, including sea lions, penguins, killer whales, and dolphins, part of your guest list. SeaWorld Orlando offers a package that includes a customized ceremony with an officiant, a harpist, the bridal bouquet, and the groom's boutonniere, as well as park passes and lunch coupons for the newlyweds and eight guests.

- Want to get married in a hot air balloon? Check out **Orange Blossom Balloons** in Lake Buena Vista, Florida. This company's standard wedding package includes transportation to the launch site, the ceremony (which takes place in the hot air balloon while it is grounded), a one-hour flight for two in a private balloon, champagne toasts on landing, a buffet breakfast, and a wedding cake.

HAVING YOUR WEDDING AT HOME

An at-home wedding can epitomize what intimate weddings are all about. However, if you plan on having your wedding at someone's home, you might have more work cut out for you than you thought—especially if it's your home and you plan to jazz it up for the occasion.

One of the first things Darin and I did after deciding to have our reception at home was hit a local nursery to load up on flowers and other bedding plants. In fact, we spent that entire spring and summer landscaping our property, which included planting hundreds of impatiens as well as an assortment of perennials.

Even though the reception would be outdoors, Darin and I decided to also fix up our house before the wedding. We stripped wallpaper, painted, stripped more wallpaper, and did I mention stripping wallpaper? Even with plenty of help from family, Darin and I busted our behinds trying to get things in order.

Of course, not all couples planning an at-home wedding spend months fixing up their homes. Some don't lift a finger on home improvements prior to the wedding. If that's the case, planning and preparing can be a lot easier.

Either way, many details need attention if you plan a wedding at home. Firstly, call your local government office to find out if construction is planned for your area around the time of your wedding. The last thing you need is a muddy, noisy, messy road on the day of your wedding.

At least a week before your wedding, let your neighbors know what's happening, and warn them of potential noise and traffic. Also, if you are having an outdoor ceremony, let your neighbors know what time it will take place, so they won't run their leaf blowers and lawn mowers during your "I dos." (Once neighbors know of your plans, they might even offer parking space or lend a hand. Our neighbors offered the use of a portable stage, which worked great for the Irish band and the emcee.)

Then you have the issue of seating. Unless you are having a tiny wedding, you'll need to rent some tables and chairs. To complete the table settings, you also may have to rent linens, glassware, and dinnerware.

Now for something entirely unglamorous: toilets. No matter where you have your wedding, you're going to need at least one. This least romantic thing about your wedding is one of the most important. If your wedding will be at someone's home, you might decide that guests can use the home's washrooms; but after some serious thought, you might change your mind. Do you really want your guests traipsing in and out of that home? Can the plumbing system take the wear and tear? Might the septic system be overstressed, causing a plumbing nightmare on the biggest day of your life? (Ever see *Meet the Parents*?)

HOW'S THE WEATHER?

Want to know about your wedding day weather in advance? Check out The United States Weather Pages planner (www.uswx.com). Simply input your wedding city and state and a date to find out whether the day in that city has historically been a rain or shine kind of day.

The last thing Darin and I wanted on our wedding day was a lawn flooded with sewage. To prevent this, we opted for a portable toilet. At first, I had reservations about it—I thought guests might think it was tacky and out of place. After doing some research, we discovered that portable toilets aren't what they used to be. New user-friendly models are made of polyplastic in pleasing colors, such as dark green, burgundy, and royal blue. Besides being more pleasing to the eye, they have sinks and flushable toilets. Even though they are more expensive than the basic models, we correctly figured they were definitely worth the splurge. We had no complaints from our guests—and, in fact, one gentleman complimented us on our "classy" portable toilets. (How's that for an oxymoron?)

Don't be afraid to take this route. You can make a portable rest room less industrial by adding a bouquet of flowers, a candle, fragrant hand soap, a good supply of paper towels, an air freshener, and lights.

A Ceremony With Sun and Sand

GAYLE AND JOHN, both Californians, wanted a casual wedding that wouldn't cost them an arm and a leg. The solution: A $6,300 wedding on a beach in California. "We really wanted to have a barefoot on the beach wedding," says Gayle.

On a warm June afternoon with the surf in the background and seagulls flying overhead, the couple stood barefoot on the sand in front of thirty-seven guests (most of whom were also shoeless) and exchanged vows they had written themselves.

After the couple was pronounced husband and wife, guests were invited to walk down to the water for a unique ritual. "The officiant asked all of the guests to follow us to the water's edge and toss rose petals into the ocean as a symbol of sharing our joy with the world, as 'the ocean is the great unifier of all faiths and all peoples,'" says Gayle. "It was so unique, so lighthearted, and playful." After the ceremony, guests headed to a nearby hotel for a buffet.

Gayle incorporated the beach theme into many wedding elements. The invitations were dolphin themed, and the favors were shell angel Christmas ornaments. Gayle also used shells to decorate for the ceremony and the reception.

However, Gayle says the ceremony needed little adornment. "I enjoyed the fact that nature provides its own wonderful decoration and requires very little extra. But, truly, the best part was the music of the waves and how we truly felt that we were in the 'original' and most profound cathedral of nature," she says.

Because the couple wanted the true beach experience—breezes and all—they did not use any form of shelter for their ceremony. But they did have a backup plan. "In the event of a storm we would have moved the ceremony inside to our reception room," says Gayle. Because they were prepared, Gayle and John didn't worry about the weather at all.

TENT TALK

A tent can provide the shelter you need and create a beautiful atmosphere for your big day, but tents can be costly—especially if you want the works (e.g., a dance floor, lighting, air-conditioning, and professional decor). If you are on a tight budget, you can opt for a tent without a dance floor and no air-conditioning, and you can decorate it yourself.

If you want to use a tent, make sure you deal with an aboveboard company that uses clean, quality tents and will set up and tear down the tent without any glitches. Look for someone—friends, acquaintances, or co-workers—who can give you a recommendation. You can even call local wedding planners. Most won't hesitate to offer referrals as long as you mention the planner's name to the rental company you hire.

Like Darin and I did, be sure to make arrangements for several local tent companies to come to your wedding site and give you an estimate. Insist that the companies each do an on-site survey. This will help determine the appropriate tent style and size, and will reveal whether the ground is sloped and whether tree branches need to be removed to make room for the tent.

We chose the company that a wedding planning professional had recommended to us. The company wasn't the least expensive one, but it reputedly provided good service and clean tents—and we weren't disappointed.

QUESTIONS TO ASK A TENT COMPANY:

- How long have you been in business?

- Are you insured?

- Are your tents clean? How old are they? Are they flame retardant?

- Do you have any tents set up on display? (Although many tent companies don't keep tents set up at their offices, ask if you can visit one of their job sites. You can see for yourself if the tents are clean and what the tent will look like.)

- Will you send someone to our site if the tent needs further anchoring due to wind, etc.?

GOING GREEN

"Green" weddings are becoming more popular. Some ways couples can have environmentally friendly weddings include:

- using cloth napkins and tablecloths

- avoiding Styrofoam or plastic glassware

- sending invitations made from recycled paper

- providing recycling bins for recyclable waste products

117

- Will we get a contract with tent setup and teardown times and dates?

- Are tent setup, teardown, and sidewalls included in the price?

THE TIME OF DAY

If you plan to get married outdoors in the summertime, keep in mind that late afternoon is the hottest part of the day. To keep the heat from getting to you and your guests, schedule your wedding for late morning or early evening.

TENT STYLES

You have three basic tent types to choose from: push-pole, frame, and tension tents. All three styles of tents have removable sidewalls, which are either plain white canvas, clear vinyl, or cathedral-window style (the most attractive). Flooring in different styles—plywood, plastic, parquet, artificial turf—can be installed inside each type of tent; this generally adds a great deal to the cost. How will you know which one is best for your wedding?

Push-Pole Tents

Push-pole tents, the most popular of the three types, offer the greatest flexibility and cost effectiveness. A push-pole tent has a ceiling that slopes from a row of center poles to a shorter series of poles then to poles on the perimeter of the tent. Their graceful peaks make these tents attractive. The tent is anchored in the ground by staking, and it generally needs seven feet (two meters) of clearance on each side. The tent's interior poles can interfere with the room inside the tent and can mean more work—unless you don't mind the look of the metal poles, you will have to cover or disguise them.

Darin and I opted for a push-pole tent with no added floor. We let our lawn serve as the carpet, and we had no regrets. However, if we had had a soggy day, it might have been a different story.

Frame Tents

Frame tents are more expensive than push-pole tents, in part because they are more time consuming to install. A frame tent's ceiling is a framework of horizontal poles, which can be distracting and not aesthetically pleasing. However, false canvas ceilings can be installed to cover the ceiling framework, and frame tents have no interior poles. Frame tents are ideal for tight spots because no clearance around the perimeter of the tent is needed and because the tents can be as little as ten feet (three meters) wide.

Tension Tents

Tension tents are the least commonly used of the three tent styles. The center poles in a tension tent are very high, so the tent has very steep slopes. The high ceiling does give the tent an open, airy feel. A tension tent has fewer interior poles than a push-pole tent has, which means more room inside the tent. Tension tents are the most stable and wind resistant of the three tent styles.

ROOM TO MOVE—AND TO GROOVE

When choosing a tent size err on the side of roominess—especially if you and your guests will sit down for a meal. Allow for enough space between tables so that when guests get up from their chairs they won't bump into guests at the next table. According to experts, a seated dinner with dancing requires about eighteen square feet (two square meters) of floor space per person.

If space is tight, consider using square tables instead of round ones, which take up more room. Also consider setting up other smaller tents for appetizers, the wedding cake and desserts, the guest book, and the bar. [Darin and I set up two ten-by-ten (three meters by three meters) fly tents (tents that have a top but no sides) to house the bar and the dessert/appetizer/cake tables.]

BUG OFF!

If you're planning an outdoor wedding for a summer month, you'll probably have a few bugs visit your festivities, and your biggest concerns will be mosquitoes and biting flies. Take all the precautions you can, and make sure you have a strong mosquito repellent handy in case all else fails!

Since Darin and I live near a lake, a marsh, and plenty of large trees, our property is a popular spot for those pests. We were both concerned about the chances of an invasion, so here's what we did for our September wedding:

- We scheduled the reception to start at 4 P.M. so that dinner would be finished before mosquito time.

- Although we don't like using pesticides, we had a professional spray the inside of the tent, the lawn, and the shrubs with pyrethrum the night before our wedding.

- We set up at least a dozen citronella torches outside of the tent.

- We bought a big container of Deep Woods OFF (the kind with a high percentage of DEET), just in case. We also had a mild repellent for the kids, who shouldn't use repellents with high concentrations of DEET.

And what happened? Not a mosquito or fly in sight—that is, until the band began to play. As soon as the music started, guests began slapping themselves silly, and not because they were digging the music. A true army of mosquitoes invaded the tent and hunted down all exposed flesh. Thankfully, the mosquito repellent came to the rescue, and everyone partied on.

TO BEE OR NOT TO BEE

Mosquitoes and flies aren't the only insects that might show up uninvited. Bees and other stinging creatures might arrive in droves. To prevent bees and other insects from landing on your edibles, consider setting food in a netted tent or keeping food indoors until serving time. Our fruit-topped wedding cake was a popular attraction for our guests—and for every bee in a ten-mile radius. Thankfully, no one at the festivities was allergic to bees.

HOW DO I LOOK?

Here's some excellent advice for any bride: Do not shop for a wedding dress until you know whether the wedding will be indoors or outdoors. In many cases, a wedding dress that is suitable for an indoor wedding would not be appropriate outdoors. For instance, a bride who will walk down a grassy aisle or along a sandy beach, should not have a mile-long train dragging behind her. If a wedding will be in the peak of summer, a dress with long sleeves and heavy fabrics is definitely not desirable.

Trial Run

If you plan to have a professional do your makeup, go for a trial run. Otherwise, you risk the added stress of not being happy with your wedding-day makeup!

The elements will impact not only everyone's comfort level but also their appearance. Heat and humidity can wreak havoc on any hairdo, as can wind. Make sure a mirror— not to mention a can of good hairspray—is accessible. Hot weather can also make for a shiny face; pressed powder is a solution—for both brides and grooms.

Speaking of makeup, natural light tends to cause makeup to look heavier. Outdoor brides might consider applying their wedding-day makeup near a window so that they can gauge how much makeup to wear.

A Ceremony in Central Park's Conservatory Garden

~

JUDY & JUSTIN

NEW YORK CITY, NEW YORK

THE MEETING:	In 1999, Justin posted a singles ad online, and Judy responded. "He drew a goofy cartoon of himself playing the guitar, and I answered his ad because of the cartoon," says Judy.
THE PROPOSAL:	Justin proposed to Judy on Valentine's Day at a cozy restaurant in Greenwich Village. After dessert, he gave Judy a card then pulled a tissue from his pocket. Inside the tissue was a dazzling diamond engagement ring. Justin placed the ring on Judy's finger then humbly popped the question. After getting over the initial surprise, Judy gave him precisely the answer he was hoping for.
CEREMONY:	Central Park's Conservatory Garden
RECEPTION:	Willow, a French restaurant in New York City
NUMBER OF GUESTS:	23
COST:	$4,525; paid for by the bride and groom
PLANNING DURATION:	7 months

Judy and Justin agreed from the start that they wanted a small wedding. "We wanted our wedding to be memorable and to know that each and every person who attended came because they loved us, not because we were going to feed them afterwards," explains Judy.

The couple decided to restrict their guest list to close friends and immediate family. Because the couple paid for their own wedding, they did not feel obligated to invite guests beyond those on that guest list. "We had full control of the wedding. Hence, we didn't get the hassle of parents who wanted Mrs. So-and-So to be added to the list. It was quite a smooth process for us," says Judy.

THE WEDDING

From the moment Judy and Justin got engaged, they had their hearts set on an outdoor wedding. "We did not want to be cooped up inside a church on a Saturday morning," says Judy.

Judy and Justin wanted to get married in Central Park, so they checked out the park's Web site (www.centralpark2000.com) and discovered that the park was home to the Conservatory Garden, a picturesque place that neither Judy nor Justin had ever heard about.

Central Park's Conservatory Garden is a lush oasis located in the northeast corner of Central Park in Manhattan. Designer Frederick Law Olmsted originally designed it as an arboretum at the end of the nineteenth century. However, during the Great Depression the buildings on the property were torn down because they were too costly to maintain, and gardens, which also fell into neglect, were planted in their place. It wasn't until the 1980s that landscape designer Lynden Miller restored the gardens.

In the gardens are sprawling green lawns, flowering shrubs and trees, artful fountains, and a rainbow assortment of vibrant annuals and perennials. On their first visit, the couple fell in love with the gardens. "We went back time and time again because it's so gorgeous!" says Judy.

The garden is divided into three sections: the French style garden, the Italianate garden, and the English garden. Judy and Justin chose to be married in the English garden—also known as the Secret Garden—which is filled with a variety of English perennials and has a bronze statue depicting two characters from the children's book *The Secret Garden* by Frances Hodgson Burnett.

Their wedding day started out cloudy, but sunshine was streaming through the trees by 11:15 A.M., the time to begin the ceremony. As friends and family gathered around the Secret Garden fountain and anticipated the couple's arrival, a guitar player softly strummed "Ode to Joy." (Although their wedding was only eleven days after the tragedy of Sept. 11, twenty-three of the twenty-five guests they invited showed up.)

Breaking with tradition, Judy and Justin walked down the aisle together. Beneath the cool shade of a tree, they said their vows, which they had written. "The vows themselves were short but sweet. Then we kissed, knowing that this was the start of a new beginning," Judy says. And then they kissed again. "Our photographer didn't get a good angle, so he made us kiss again! Everyone laughed at that," says Judy.

Because the Conservatory Garden is open to the public, the couple had a few unexpected "guests." "We had tourists and neighborhood residents alike peeking around the hedges at us during the ceremony and walking up to us before and after to say congratulations. It was something we didn't anticipate, but we didn't mind it either. I'm glad we helped people get their minds off Sept. 11, if at least for a few minutes," says Judy.

Although Judy and Justin did not have any shelter from the elements, they had made a backup plan in case of inclement weather: Their minister had offered to lend them his chapel in case of rain. "Thankfully, we didn't need to use it," says Judy.

The couple originally wanted an outdoor reception too, but they learned that the Conservatory Garden does not allow outdoor receptions. The couple's reception was held instead at Willow, a New York City restaurant where they indulged in a three-course meal.

What was the best thing about having an intimate wedding? "An intimate wedding allows you to mingle with each and every guest without having that whirlwind feeling that brides . . . whose wedding entailed over one hundred guests [talk about]," says Judy.

According to Judy, another advantage of having an intimate wedding is that it will make you feel more at ease than a large wedding with people you don't know well. "With only your loved ones as your guests, you don't feel nervous. You don't feel like you're putting on a show for a crowd of semistrangers. You can truly act like yourself and not worry about things that can go wrong! I honestly went through that entire day not feeling any anxiety, and that was a definite plus to an already beautiful day!" Judy says.

Judy and Justin's Wedding Budget

Reception venue, food, and beverages (including cake and service)	$1,600
Attire	$1,230
Flowers	$180
Photography	$300
Stationery	$160
Gifts	$70
Wedding rings	$390
Ceremony	$515
Miscellaneous expenses (decorations for reception and marriage license)	$80
Total	**$4,525**

CHAPTER 8

What's the Theme?

In her pretty white wedding dress and veil, here comes a traditional bride.

Not until the guests see her walking down the aisle do they realize she's

definitely not conventional. Instead of plain white wedding shoes, she has

on her feet red shoes—glittering ruby-red slippers, just like the ones

Dorothy wore. And the maid of honor is wearing fairy wings and carrying

a wand; the flower girls and ring bearer are dressed like Munchkins, and

the officiant resembles a wizard.

If you're a creative type who loves to do things a bit differently,

a theme wedding might be just what you're after. Theme weddings are

a great way to let your personality shine through, to bring out your

playfulness and creativity.

PLANNING A THEME WEDDING

Keeping your wedding intimate will make your theme wedding easier to pull off. If you have a historical theme, for instance, it's much easier to get forty guests to arrive in period attire than two hundred. Besides, it's more likely that all the guests at a small wedding will know you well enough to accept your wedding style and be more willing to play along.

Although there is usually more planning involved with a theme wedding—especially if you carry your theme over to everything from the food to the favors—keeping your guest list small will also help reduce your planning time. It's easier to wrap 40 favors than 240!

Since having a small wedding means you have more location choices, you'll be more likely to find one that fits the theme. If you have a historical theme, you have a better chance of finding a museum or historical site if your guest list is not huge. For a nautical theme, it will be easier to find a boat to accommodate seventy-five than one that will fit three hundred.

Then there's the issue of cost: Having an elaborate theme wedding can be expensive. A Victorian wedding, complete with period attire, decor, musicians, food, and other wedding details can be expensive. However, if you have only thirty on your guest list, you might pull it off for less than a large wedding without any unusual touches.

As mentioned earlier, an intimate wedding means you can get your guests involved. One way to do this is to have them arrive in costume—perfect for a masquerade ball, a historical theme, or a Halloween wedding. (If you go this route, make sure you let guests know of costume rental places. Also offer suggestions on what they should wear. Someone invited to a medieval wedding, for example, might not have a clue about clothing worn during that period.)

You can also have your guests participate in the wedding. For instance, if you choose to have a reenactment during a historically themed wedding, you can encourage each guest to play a part. At an Easter-themed wedding, you might have both your adult and younger guests enjoy a scavenger hunt during the reception.

Guests can also help decorate. What about a pumpkin carving party the night before a Halloween wedding so you'll have fresh centerpieces? How about a tree-trimming get-together the night before a Christmas-themed wedding? What about gathering guests the day before the wedding to decorate eggs to be placed in baskets at an Easter wedding?

CHOOSING A THEME

When it comes to choosing a theme, the possibilities are endless. You can derive inspiration from so many sources: favorite movies; a favorite season or holiday; an era, such as the roaring twenties or the fabulous fifties or, for real history buffs, medieval, Renaissance, or Victorian periods. Vocations and hobbies can make ideal themes. An artist, for instance, might choose an art-themed wedding at an art gallery. A fireman might have his wedding at a firehouse and arrive with his bride on a fire truck. A dog lover might have a canine-friendly wedding in a park.

Of course, inspiration can come from less-obvious places. Keely used her grandmother's garnet jewelry to spark her imagination. "The theme started with my grandmother's garnet jewelry that she got on her wedding day from my grandfather. The jewelry included a large oval locket with garnets and a large oval ring set with garnets . . . so garnet became the color, and the theme turned into one of old-fashioned elegance," says Keely.

BREAKING WITH TRADITION

More and more brides and grooms are looking for ways to make their nuptials unique. They don't want their weddings to be just like so many other weddings.

Depending on how far you want to go, theme weddings can take quite a bit of research and planning—even if a wedding is small. Some couples choose to incorporate just a few elements of a particular theme. Other couples go all the way, using the theme in everything from the wedding meal to the tablecloths.

The Internet is a great resource for couples planning weddings around a theme. Not only is merchandise—everything from stationery to favors—available online, plenty of advice is available, too. The Web site www.weddingthemes.com offers detailed information on everything from medieval weddings to beach weddings, and it has message boards where couples share information about their weddings. Another source for theme ideas is www.askginka.com/themes; it has five hundred of them.

HOLIDAY THEMES

For some couples, there's no better time to celebrate their nuptials than around a favorite holiday. Whether it's during the Christmas season or on Valentine's Day, a holiday wedding can be a truly memorable occasion.

TIPS FOR PLANNING A HOLIDAY WEDDING

- Book early. Venues book up fast for the holidays.

- Find out if the venue will be decorated for the holiday of your theme. If so, you might save a bundle on decorations.

- Let guests know about the wedding date well in advance. Holidays are a busy time, so let your guests mark your wedding date on their calendars before something else comes up. If guests will come in from out of town, it's best for them to know well in advance so they can book airline tickets before the holiday rush.

NEW YEAR'S EVE

Balloons. Kazoos. Party hats. Sparklers. Fireworks. Champagne. Wedding cake? Some couples can imagine no better way to ring in the new year than with a wedding celebration. Here are some suggestions for making it part of your nuptials:

- **Stationery**: Purchase or create invitations with images of fireworks, party hats, or the numerals of the upcoming year.

- **Decor:** Decorate with oodles of balloons and streamers.

- **Colors**: Choose black and silver for your wedding colors.

- **Food**: Choose party foods, including plenty of hors d'oeuvres. Since your wedding will probably start later than usual (8 or 9 P.M. is the suggested time), why not simply have a cocktail reception? Put sparklers on your wedding cake, and make sure you've got some bubbly on hand for when the clock strikes midnight!

- **Favors**: Give guests kazoos, party hats, and new calendars.

VALENTINE'S DAY

Hearts, red roses, chocolate, amore: Valentine's Day is the one day each year when we are expected to embrace romance and remind our sweeties just how much we adore them. Not a bad time of year for saying "I do"! Here are some ways to bring the Valentine's Day theme into your nuptials.

- ☙ **Stationery**: Purchase or create invitations with a red rose or heart motif, or purchase heart-shaped cards. Attach place cards to a single red rose.

- ☙ **Decor**: Decorate with heart-shaped helium balloons. Place red rose bouquets on each table. Cherubs can also be a part of the decor.

- ☙ **Colors**: Choose red, black, and white for your wedding colors.

- ☙ **Food**: Have a heart-shaped wedding cake.

- ☙ **Favors**: Give guests cherubs or heart-shaped soap or picture frames, or boxes of candy.

EASTER

Bunny rabbits are busy making baby bunnies. Green shoots are forcing their way out of the soil. The Earth is coming alive again. Women in light spring dresses rejoice in the warm air. Children with happy faces run through the cool grass looking for shining treasures. It's not just the arrival of spring that has everyone in good spirits; it's Easter time. Easter is one of the most vibrant times of the year, and it's a great time for tying the knot. Its message of rebirth is perfectly suited for saying "I do."

Aside from the pretty, soft colors of the season, all the other things we equate with Easter—daffodils, lilies, colored eggs, chocolate—can also tie in well with a wedding. Here are some ideas to make the holiday fit in with your nuptials:

- ☙ **Stationery**: Use invitations with Easter symbols, such as spring chicks, bunnies, or flowers. Instead of using place cards, write guests' names on colored eggs and place those in eggcups.

- ☙ **Decor**: If you will get married in a church, chances are it will already be filled with Easter lilies. For the reception venue, use daffodils, tulips, irises, or Easter lilies as centerpieces. If you don't want floral centerpieces, fill elegant glass bowls with colored eggs or fill a basket with chocolate eggs.

- ☙ **Colors**: Choose pale green, mauve, light blue, and pale yellow as wedding colors.

- ☙ **Food**: Ham and scalloped potatoes go hand in hand with the holiday. Use small chocolate eggs or Easter bunnies to decorate the wedding cake, or have the cake made in an egg shape.

⊛ **Favors**: Give guests small baskets filled with delicious Easter chocolate, or give out hand-painted eggs.

HALLOWEEN

Think back to when you were a kid. Wasn't it a blast to get dressed up and trick-or-treat? Wasn't it great fun to get spooked by scary houses and creepy props? The ghoulish charm of Halloween doesn't have to disappear with adulthood. In fact, many folks consider it the number one holiday of the year. There's no doubt that creating a Halloween-themed wedding can be a lot of fun—especially for those with a mischievous spirit. Here are some wickedly fun ideas to make Halloween part of your nuptials:

⊛ **Stationery**: Use invitations shaped like jack-o'-lanterns or printed with images of witches, ghosts, or other ghastly creatures. Another option is to have the invitations printed with a Halloween candy pattern.

⊛ **Decor**: Use as centerpieces jack-o'-lanterns or glass bowls with black marbles and floating orange candles. If you want floral centerpieces, use black silk roses. Place candelabras and orange twinkle lights throughout the venue.

⊛ **Colors**: For your wedding colors, choose orange and black, of course.

⊛ **Food**: Serve pumpkin pie for dessert. For cocktails, serve Bloody Marys and zombies. Have a wedding cake shaped like a pumpkin.

⊛ **Favors**: Give guests small goodie bags filled with Halloween candy.

CHRISTMAS

Imagine sitting around a crackling fire with dear friends and family while Christmas tree lights cast a warm glow on cheerful faces, and the halls are decked with yuletide cheer and smelling like fresh gingerbread, cinnamon, evergreen, and cranberries. Despite all the hustle and bustle of the season, Christmastime for many is one of the most enjoyable times of the year. Why not make it even more enjoyable by celebrating a life event? Here are some ideas for a Christmas-themed wedding:

Ho, Ho, Ho

Want to throw a wonderful surprise into your Christmas wedding? Have Santa Claus make an appearance to hand out favors from his gift sack or get your guests out on the dance floor. He could even act as the deejay, or the emcee.

- **Stationery**: Use a Christmas motif (you have so many to choose from!) on your invitations, or send invitations that look like Christmas cards.

- **Decor**: Decorate with snowflakes, small Christmas trees, angels, garland, poinsettias, evergreen, holly, and twinkle lights. For centerpieces, fill bowls with shiny Christmas ball ornaments, or use poinsettias or rosemary plants (the ones shaped like Christmas trees). Cut or live Christmas trees will make the venue smell amazing!

- **Colors**: Choose red, green, silver, and gold as your wedding colors.

- **Food**: Serve comfort foods, such as soups and pastas, as well as foods associated with the time of year—roast turkey and stuffing, shortbread, gingerbread, and cranberry squares.

- **Favors**: Give your guests homemade gingerbread men, a Christmas ornament, or some other Christmas decoration, or stuff miniature stockings with chocolate and other goodies.

A Christmas Wedding at The Wrigley Mansion

LYNETTE AND CHARLES went all out for their Christmas-themed wedding. "We decided to have a small wedding because we wanted to have a really nice event," says Lynette. Their December wedding, which had seventy-one attendees, cost around $25,000.

The couple resides in Chicago, but both of them are from Phoenix, Arizona. They chose to say their vows at a Presbyterian church in Paradise Valley, Arizona, and have a brunch reception at The Wrigley Mansion Club in Phoenix.

The mansion was built between 1929 and 1931 by William Wrigley Jr., of Wrigley Chewing Gum fame, as a fiftieth anniversary gift to his wife. It has twenty-four rooms, seventeen bathrooms, and eleven fireplaces; and it offers a dramatic view of the Valley of the Sun, downtown Phoenix, and Camelback Mountain. "It is a gorgeous location, and during Christmas, the mansion is decorated beautifully," says Lynette. "This was attractive to us because, although the price per person was somewhat high, we could save a lot on decor." Huge Christmas trees, a gingerbread mansion, poinsettia plants, and garland were placed throughout the venue.

While guests sipped on spiced cider during the cocktail hour, four Dickens carolers the couple had hired for the occasion stood by a Christmas tree in the living room and sang carols.

Tables were dressed with burgundy damask tablecloths and cream napkins tied with gold tassels. The centerpieces were bouquets of white roses and Christmas ornaments. The couple had a sweetheart table instead of a head table, and it was dressed with a cream tablecloth, gold napkins, and a dark burgundy rose centerpiece.

For guest favors, the couple gave votive candles in various Christmas scents. The favors, each in a burgundy wicker sleigh trimmed with balsam fur and red berries, served as place cards.

The couple agreed that they couldn't have chosen a better time of year for their wedding. "We enjoyed having a Christmas-themed wedding because it is such a festive time of year and most people are in good spirits," says Lynette. "It was a blast to plan, because Christmas items and ideas are plentiful!"

THE SEASONS

Instead of focusing on a favorite holiday, some couples might plan a wedding based on their most cherished season. Winter enthusiasts might wed in a winter wonderland, while lovers of spring might choose a garden theme. Couples who adore the fall might have a harvest-themed wedding, complete with a hayride at a pumpkin patch.

SPRING

Think of spring. Do you see robins? Buds on trees? Tulips and daffodils poking up from flower beds? The browns and grays of winter have finally been washed away and painted over with vibrant colors. The sun's warmth has dissolved the chill in the air. Neighbors that you haven't seen all winter wave to you from their gardens. Children wearing bright windbreakers ride by on bicycles. Associated with new life, freshness, energy, and rebirth, spring is a wonderful season in which to tie the knot. Can there be a more cheerful season to say "I do"? Here are a few ideas to make it part of your wedding:

- **Stationery**: Use spring motifs, such as spring flowers, on your stationery.

- **Decor**: Use daffodils, irises, and tulips in your bouquets and centerpieces.

- **Colors**: For decorating, go with cool pastels, such as pale greens, blues, yellows, and mauves. Have your attendants wear pretty spring dresses in pastel colors.

- **Food**: Choose light spring fare, such as fresh garden salads and lightly grilled vegetables, to accompany the main course. Serve refreshing white wine.

- **Favors**: Give your guests spring bouquets, seed packets, or flower bulbs.

SUMMER

Sunny skies, warm breezes, sprawling green lawns, gardens bursting with life—no wonder the majority of weddings are held in the summer. There are several ways to incorporate the many splendors of the season into your nuptials.

A **garden theme** allows you to make full use of all the gorgeous flowers of the season—especially if you have an outdoor wedding. Here are some suggestions for incorporating a garden theme:

- ❧ **Stationery**: Use pressed flowers on your invitations and place cards.

- ❧ **Decor**: Use brightly colored garden flowers for your bouquets. Use them for your centerpieces as well, or use potted plants. Wear flowers in your hair, and make flower halos for your flower girls.

- ❧ **Colors**: Use bright, cheerful colors, such as coral, mint, pink, and lavender.

- ❧ **Food**: Take advantage of all the great fruits and veggies that are in season.

- ❧ **Favors**: Give your guests handmade garden soap or pressed flowers behind glass.

For many couples, the beach is a romantic place. There are many ways to bring a **beach theme** into a wedding—even if your wedding location is landlocked. Here are some ideas:

- ❧ **Stationery**: Use seashell, water, or sun motifs for your invitations.

- ❧ **Decor**: Use sand and shells when decorating. Candles in sand-filled jars, for instance, make great centerpieces. Tiki torches can add drama to evening weddings on the beach.

- ❧ **Colors**: Use bright, tropical colors, or stick with crisp linen shades.

- ❧ **Food**: After the ceremony, celebrate with a clambake or a barbecue. Chocolate seashells added to the wedding cake are a nice touch.

- ❧ **Favors**: Give guests small galvanized beach pails filled with chocolate kisses or votive candles.

AUTUMN

Do you love the sound of autumn leaves crunching beneath your feet? What about the sight of sugar maples blushing bright crimson under a blue sky or the smell of a forest when its floor is covered with fallen leaves? If so, an autumn theme might be just right for your wedding. Here are some ideas for an autumn theme:

- **Stationery**: Leaves are a lovely motif for autumn weddings. You can use them on your invitations and place cards.

- **Decor**: For centerpieces, you can use autumn leaves, Indian corn, gourds, squash, bittersweet, and small pumpkins. If you prefer floral centerpieces, place fall flowers, such as mums and hydrangeas, in baskets.

- **Colors**: Have your attendants wear fall colors, such as wine, navy, rust, orange, or hunter green. Use the same colors in your decor.

- **Food**: Serve harvest foods, such as butternut squash soup, turkey with stuffing, and pumpkin pie.

- **Favors**: Give your guests cinnamon and apple potpourri, small bottles of maple syrup, or maple sugar.

WINTER

Snowflakes falling in moonlight. Pine branches covered in fresh, glittering snow. Icicles on rooftops. A frozen lake, smooth as glass. For some, wintertime provides the ideal backdrop for a wedding. Having a wedding around a crackling fire is a sure way to give everyone the warm fuzzies, especially if eggnog or mulled cider is served. Here are some ways to make the wintertime part of your event:

- **Stationery**: Use a snowflake motif in your invitations, or have them covered with white glitter.

- **Decor**: Decorate the venue with snowflakes, pine boughs, holly, cranberries, and twinkle lights. Use small evergreen trees or floating cranberry-scented candles as centerpieces.

- **Colors**: Choose pale blue, silver, and gold.

- **Food**: Serve delicious comfort foods, such as prime rib, potatoes, pasta, and decadent chocolate desserts.

- **Favors**: Give your guests snow globes, silver bells, or pine-scented candles.

WINTER SPORTS BUFF

Some winter sports enthusiasts chose to incorporate their favorite sport into their nuptials. Couples have been known to get married on ski slopes and on ice rinks.

133

IT'S HISTORY

If you're nostalgic for a particular era, why not make it part of your wedding? You don't have to be a history buff to pull it off; you just have to be willing to do some research. The library and the Internet are great places to start looking for information on a particular era. Many historical societies maintain a Web presence (simply do a search under "historical societies") and would be happy to provide you with information. Also, check out the Resources section at the back of this book for Web sites.

You could also chose a more recent era for your wedding, such as the fifties or sixties. If you really have a sense of humor, you might use the seventies.

MEDIEVAL

Imagine getting married on horseback with a castle as your backdrop. Imagine the two of you—not to mention all of your guests—dressed in period attire as you indulge in a medieval feast. Imagine hearing tranquil medieval tunes from a harp and flute as you and your honey sneak off for a few smooches beneath lantern light.

The medieval theme seems to be popular for weddings, and numerous Web sites provide information on medieval weddings. You can even join a medieval and Renaissance wedding ring at www.midnightgarden.com/wedding/mrwring.html. Personal Web sites created by couples who have had medieval-themed weddings are another great resource. Simply type "our medieval wedding" in your favorite search engine to find some of them. Here are some ideas to get you started on your medieval wedding:

- **Stationery**: Use calligraphy on the invitations and send them as scrolls, or accent the invitations with castles, knights, or Celtic patterns. Use medieval wording.

- **Decor**: Use ivy to decorate the reception venue, and use candles for centerpieces. Create a medieval effect by using lanterns throughout the venue. If you're really ambitious, make a cardboard or wood cutout castle to use as a prop behind the head table.

- **Colors**: Choose wine, hunter green, black, brown, and silver as wedding colors.

- **Food**: Serve a medieval feast of venison, beef, pheasant, parsnips, soups, salads, custard pie, and mulled wine. The feast may well be a highlight of your wedding!

⊛ **Favors:** Give guests brass bells tied with ribbon, nosegays, lace pockets filled with potpourri or dried lavender, or beeswax candles.

VICTORIAN

Perhaps the romance and elegance of the Victorian era have always been a source of inspiration to you. Maybe the lavish fashions and decorum of the upper class and the era's penchant for good manners, modesty, and self-restraint pique your interest.

For a glimpse into the Victorian era, check out any of dozens of movies set during this time period, including *The Age of Innocence* and *An Ideal Husband*. The Internet is also a great place to find information. Check out the Resources section at the back of this book for Web sites. Here are some suggestions on making this era of elegance part of your "I dos."

⊛ **Stationery:** Send elegant formal invitations that have cameos or lacy borders. Make fan-shaped programs.

⊛ **Decor:** Use roses, baby's breath, or orange blossoms placed in teapots as centerpieces. Surround the teapots with teacups filled with water and floating votives. Use bows, pearls, and lace when decorating.

⊛ **Colors:** Use ivory, gold, and rose as the wedding colors.

⊛ **Food:** Have an afternoon tea with hors d'oeuvres.

⊛ **Favors:** Give your guests small teacups filled with peppermints, or give them dried lavender sachets or fans.

ROARING TWENTIES

Jazz music plays at a smoke-filled speakeasy, while lipsticked women in flapper dresses dance the Charleston with men in dark suits. It's the roaring twenties—the era of Prohibition and the Mob. *The Great Gatsby* enthusiasts and anyone else fascinated by this era will have a ball re-creating it for a wedding. Go online to find out more about this time period. The Web site www.reasontoparty.com/roaringtwenties.htm offers a variety of ideas on hosting a roaring twenties party. Many of the suggestions can be applied to a wedding. Here are some more ideas:

⊛ **Stationery:** Send invitations that have jazz motifs. Include a password for the guests to use to get into the speakeasy reception.

- ☙ **Decor**: Make the venue look like a speakeasy by using low lighting and minimal color. Use velvet tablecloths and seat covers, and use candles as centerpieces. Use palms and Boston ferns as part of the decor.

- ☙ **Colors**: Choose black, white, and gray as the wedding colors and use red accents.

- ☙ **Meal**: Serve old-fashioned cocktails and hors d'oeuvres instead of a full meal.

- ☙ **Favors**: Give your guests small bottles of "bootlegged" wine, or CDs of twenties music.

REGIONAL OR CULTURAL THEMES

No matter what your roots are—Scottish, Irish, African, Cajun, Texan, Chinese . . . — you can make your heritage part of your wedding. A cultural wedding can be lots of fun, and because it involves your ancestry, it can have special meaning.

That said, a particular culture or region does not have to be part of your heritage for you to use it as a theme for your wedding. Many couples simply fall in love with a particular place or culture and want to make it part of their wedding day. If you don't have relatives who can give you information about the culture you're interested in, check the library or the Internet (see Resources, page 184). Here are just a few examples of cultural/regional themes:

IRISH

Many North Americans adore Irish culture, especially the music, the dancing, and the beverages—all part of the fun-loving spirit of the Irish. But there's a great deal more to this culture than having a good time. Along with the rich history of Ireland, the country abounds with superstitions, customs, and folklore that are perfect additions to a wedding. Here are some other suggestions:

- ☙ **Stationery**: Send pale green invitations bearing Celtic motifs, such as the Claddagh (an Irish symbol of two hands holding a heart underneath a crown or fleur-de-lis) or shamrocks or horseshoes. Include an Irish blessing or poem in the invitation.

- ☙ **Decor**: Use bouquets of wildflowers or shamrocks as centerpieces. Decorate with ivy and other greenery, as well as green helium balloons.

- ❧ **Colors:** Choose green, ivory, and wine as your wedding colors.

- ❧ **Food:** Serve Irish fare, such as beef and stout casserole, corned beef and cabbage, Irish meatballs, Irish stew, and Bailey's Irish Cream mocha cheesecake. Have a wedding cake made in the shape of a shamrock.

- ❧ **Favors:** Give your guests picture frames with a Celtic pattern, shamrock-shaped candy containers, potted shamrock plants, mint green handmade shamrock-shaped soap, or shamrock-shaped candles.

JAPANESE

Sushi, sake, samurai, sumi-e painting, Zen, origami, bonsai, and rock gardens are just a few parts of Japanese culture. Go online for information on rituals, customs, and the history of Japanese weddings. Here are more ideas incorporating a Japanese theme:

- ❧ **Stationery:** Use fancy Japanese paper for your invitations, fold your invitations into origami shapes, or use paper fans as your invitations.

- ❧ **Decor:** Use bonsai trees or Japanese flower arrangements as centerpieces. Use paper Japanese lanterns throughout the venue, along with bamboo, paper umbrellas, and paper fans. String paper cranes throughout the venue.

- ❧ **Colors:** Use red, white, and gold as your wedding colors.

- ❧ **Food:** Provide an hors d'oeuvres table with fruits and vegetables carved into shapes. Serve sushi, sake, teriyaki, and other Japanese fare. Offer guests the choice of chopsticks or silverware. Also serve tea!

- ❧ **Favors:** Give your guests origami pieces, fortune cookies, or Japanese candy. Wrap the favors beautifully in a box.

MEXICAN

Bright colors, hot food, and salsa music. If you love to kick up your heels and are passionate about having fun, why not choose a wedding with a Mexican theme? Here are some suggestions.

- **Stationery**: Send invitations with Mexican motifs, such as chili peppers, sombreros, or cacti.

- **Decor**: For your centerpieces, fill bowls with bright red chili peppers. Use a cactus in a terra-cotta pot, or use mini piñatas. Decorate the venue with brightly colored balloons and large piñatas.

- **Colors**: Use bright shades of red, orange, and yellow for your wedding colors.

- **Food**: For appetizers, serve nachos, salsa, and quesadillas. For the main course, serve tacos, enchiladas, fajitas, and burritos. For cocktails, serve sangria, margaritas, and Mexican beer. Have a cake made in the shape of a sombrero or a cactus.

- **Favors**: Bottles of hot sauce or fancy jars of crushed and dried chili peppers make unique favors. For sweeter favors, give cellophane bags full of jelly beans in flavors such as margarita, jalapeno, and lemon lime (see www.jellybelly.com) or give tequila-flavored lollipops—complete with a worm (see www.hotlix.com/wormpops.htm)! Microwave tortilla warmers (see www.latortillaloca.com), miniature piñatas stuffed with goodies, or jars of homemade salsa also fit this theme.

MARDI GRAS

What's the first thing you associate with New Orleans? If you're like most people, you think of Mardi Gras. You don't have to get married in New Orleans to use this festive occasion as a theme for you wedding. All you need is some creativity and the willingness to have a ton of fun! Here are some suggestions:

- **Stationery**: Send invitations with a jester or mask motif.

- **Decor**: For centerpieces, fill bowls with Mardi Gras beads, or use candles in Mardi Gras colors. To decorate, buy balloons in Mardi Gras colors. Place lanterns throughout the venue.

- **Colors**: Choose purple, green, and gold as your wedding colors.

- **Food**: Serve Louisiana crab cakes for starters. Anything Cajun can be your main course—how about some blackened catfish, crawfish pasta, or jambalaya? Serve a

King Cake for dessert (see www.mardigrasstore.com/catalog/king_cakes/index .html), and have your wedding cake made in the shape of a jester, mask, or something whimsical.

WESTERN

Strong horses. Cowboys and cowgirls. Open fields and killer sunsets. There's no doubt the West has an aura of romance around it. Even if you've never set foot on a cattle ranch or ridden a horse through a Montana meadow, you might be fond of the images the West brings to mind. Here are some ideas:

- **Stationery:** Send invitations with Western motifs such as horses, cowboy hats, and barns, or create a "wanted" poster as your invitation.

- **Decor:** Use loosely arranged wildflowers or place daisies in metal buckets or mason jars for centerpieces. Use bales of hay inside the reception area. Place ropes, cowboy boots and hats, saddles, and other Western gear throughout the venue. Cover tables in red and white picnic gingham.

- **Colors:** Use blue, white, and brown as your wedding colors.

- **Food:** Serve a down-home meal of hearty foods such as roast beef and potatoes, or better yet, have a Texas barbecue, a picnic, or a pig roast. Have your wedding cake made in the shape of a cowboy boot or hat.

- **Favors:** Give your guests chocolates shaped like cowboy boots, or give them miniature cowbells, mini feed bags filled with almonds, or miniature cowboy hats filled with jelly beans.

A Western Wedding in the California Desert

AIMEE AND AL chose an old movie set, called Pioneertown, in southeastern California as the place for their Western-themed nuptials. Pioneertown was built in the high desert of California in 1946 as a set for western shows that included *The Cisco Kid, Annie Oakley, Range Rider* and *Buffalo Bill Jr.* The movie set provided a place for the actors to live—their houses were used as part of the set—and many of the buildings remain as they were when the town was conceived. Original investors in the town include Roy Rogers, Dick Curtis, and Bud Abbott.

Aimee and Al chose a wedding with a Western theme because they wanted something different and fun. They also wanted a theme that retained the seriousness of their commitment to each other. "We wanted to preserve the importance of our faith and the vows we were making," says Aimee.

The couple said their vows at Pioneertown Church, a church on the premises. Aimee wore an old-fashioned Western dress she found on the clearance rack at a Western clothing store; Al wore blue jeans, a white shirt, a suede vest, and a brown wool frock coat. He also wore a hat, boots, spurs, and a sheriff's badge.

Just before the traditional ceremony, which was held outdoors on the church porch, a friend of the couple entertained the guests by singing Clint Black and Mark Wills songs. The guests sat on bales of hay that served as pews.

The maid of honor arrived in a horse-drawn carriage. The bride, who also arrived in a horse-drawn carriage, then made her grand entrance. Following the ceremony, music from famous westerns, including *Rawhide*, *Bonanza*, and *High Noon*, played as guests posed for pictures. A horse-drawn carriage took the couple on a short trip down a dirt road to the reception, which was held at a rollicking saloon called Pappy and Harriet's Pioneertown Palace. "It's a country, 'we're family here' type of atmosphere and a local legend. It fit well with the theme," says Aimee, adding that the restaurant attracts a slew of desert regulars.

Aimee had fun planning her wedding and got plenty of help from friends and family. The couple made most of the Western-themed items themselves. They found ideas and supplies on the Internet, at country/Western stores, and at major department stores. Aimee found some glass potpourri dishes on clearance at a department store. For centerpieces, she simply filled them with water and floating candles. For favors, Aimee and her mom placed rose-shaped candies on a stick into small, colored antique medicine bottle replicas. "Most of the stuff we made ourselves because we couldn't find what we wanted. It was more work that way, but it saved us a lot of money," says Aimee.

VIVA LAS VEGAS

CRAZY ABOUT ELVIS?

Many chapels in Las Vegas will help you make this legend part of your big day. Some packages involve having "Elvis" pick you up, drive you to the chapel, perform the ceremony, and entertain you and your guests during the reception.

If you want a theme wedding without the hassle of planning all the details, head to Las Vegas. Several chapels in Las Vegas offer theme-wedding packages—and they don't all involve Elvis impersonators.

Viva Las Vegas Wedding Chapel offers more than twenty themes, including the Harley theme (which includes the rental of two Harley Davidsons for a couple of hours), The Graveyard Special (which gives you a cemetery setting complete with fog and even ghouls), and the James Bond theme (the ceremony is performed by none other than 007 himself). Most of the packages include the chapel fee, a video of the ceremony, basic flower and photo packages, and limo service to and from the wedding chapel.

Aside from the themes detailed in this chapter, you can base wedding themes on favorite sports, hobbies, vocations, movies, animals, flowers—just about anything you can imagine. Here are a few more theme ideas:

- *African Safari*: Have animal-print tablecloths, invite guests to wear safari attire, provide African food and music, and use safari-themed centerpieces and favors.

- *Alice in Wonderland*: Why not have a tea party? Use cutouts of *Alice in Wonderland* characters such as the White Rabbit and the Cheshire Cat in your decor.

- *Aquatic*: Love being on the water? Get married on a boat, and use elements from the sea in your decor.

- *Baseball*: Tie the knot on a baseball diamond, give baseball-shaped chocolates as favors, and have your wedding cake made in the shape of a bat and ball.

- *Carnival*: Still a kid at heart? Rent carnival games, cotton candy machines, snow cone makers, and other fun items to give your wedding a carnival feel.

- *Cars*: Are you and your sweetie car buffs? Arrive in your favorite car, use model cars in your decor, and have the wedding cake made in the shape of a car.

- *Cinderella*: Decorate with magic wands, crowns, and miniature castles—and remember the glass slippers!

- *Daisies*: Use daisies in all of your bouquets and centerpieces, and place candy daisies on top of your wedding cake. Give seed packets of daisies as favors.

- *Golf*: Have the wedding at a golf and country club. Give golf balls personalized with your names and wedding date as favors. Have a wedding cake in the shape of a golf course.

- *Motorcycles*: If you two are motorcycle enthusiasts and your friends are bikers too, have a motorcycle procession through town. Use the Harley Davidson colors—orange and black in decor—and have a wedding cake in the shape of a motorcycle

- *Zoo*: Some zoos open their doors to couples for weddings. Use animal motifs in the decor and tropical plants for centerpieces. Hang vines along the walls and use a paw print pattern on your stationery.

© 2001 GENE KEENUM

A Medieval Wedding

~

MELLINDA & RONDELL

DURHAM, NORTH CAROLINA

THE MEETING:	The couple met at work a little more than a year before they married. "Rondell would come by my office and give my office mate and me a hard time," says Mellinda. Eventually the two began exchanging e-mails, and the rest is history.
THE PROPOSAL:	The couple was visiting friends in Washington, DC, when Rondell placed the ring on Mellinda's finger. "Some time around 6:30 A.M., Rondell snuck into my room and put the engagement ring on my finger (he claims he didn't want to give me an opportunity to refuse). I, of course, slept through the whole thing," says Mellinda. When Mellinda woke up during the night, she noticed the ring. "I wandered into the room in which he was sleeping, crawled onto the bed, and held my hand in front of his face and said something like, 'Is this you? Did you do this?'" says Mellinda. "His response was to grin really big and say, 'Yes, will you marry me?' I, still mostly asleep, said yes."
CEREMONY & RECEPTION:	Property owned by friends of the couple.
NUMBER OF GUESTS:	57
COST:	$5,285; paid for by the bride and groom with some contributions from family and friends
PLANNING DURATION:	6 to 7 months

History buffs Mellinda and Rondell knew from the onset that they wanted a wedding with a historical theme. "Neither of us [was] impressed by formal weddings where the guests are bored, no one is sure which fork to use, and the whole thing is focused on thirty minutes worth of activity," says Mellinda.

After doing some research, they found the medieval period to be a perfect fit. The couple planned to have their wedding in the middle of May and wanted the costumes to be as comfortable as possible. "This automatically precluded anything with corsets, so we decided on the medieval time period. The dresses [were] simpler, both genders could get away with wearing one layer, and the designs [were] fairly 'airy,' so there would be some circulation," explains Mellinda. Their decision was fortuitous; the wedding-day temperature ended up being 90°!

Costumes played a big role for not only the couple but also their guests, who were asked to arrive in period attire. "We knew that if we had a costumed, themed wedding where the guests were required to wear costumes as well, we wouldn't have to worry about having too many people attend," says Mellinda. "Those that would come would have a great time, and those who felt uncomfortable about the whole concept would have an out of not being able to find a costume."

For help with planning a medieval wedding, Mellinda turned to the Internet. "I was able to get ideas from other couples who had had similar weddings, [and I got] historical information found on costume Web sites, archeological Web sites, and The Society for Creative Anachronism Web site," says Mellinda.

IN THE BOONIES

The wedding was held under a large tent in what Mellinda calls "the boondocks." There was no running water, and "a very noisy generator" was the sole source of electricity. "Rondell and I spent most of the previous two weeks getting the location ready, which included cutting a swath through the bush so that there would be a place for the tents, a clear path to the Port-a-Potties, and easy access to parking," says Mellinda. "It was worth it in the end, but [it was] a lot of work."

The couple placed tiki torches around the main tent to help keep the bugs at bay and to provide mood lighting. They also placed white Christmas lights around the inside edge of the tent so that there would be light inside the tent as it grew dark. A small, separate tent was used as the cook tent.

THE CEREMONY

An altar and a stage were set up at one end of the tent for the early-evening ceremony. Rows of wooden chairs were set up to face the stage. As guests took their places for the ceremony, Mellinda's sister-in-law helped set the mood by playing period music on her clarinet.

Once the minister took his place, the groom, who was dressed as a medieval lord with black leather lace-up boots, a lace-up shirt, a green velvet tunic, and a sword, entered on horseback. Also on horse back, his best man entered with him. Mellinda, wearing a gold, long-sleeved dress, and her maid of honor, dressed in a green, full-length dress with velvet and gold trim, also arrived on horseback. (Mellinda made both of the dresses, and in her spare time, she rides, trains, and shows Arabian horses.)

The men dismounted from their horses, they helped the two women dismount, and the ceremony began. According to Mellinda, the ceremony was fairly simple: It included the exchanging of vows and rings, the lighting of the unity candle, and communion. The vows were a combination of several different medieval wedding vows along with some of Mellinda's own words.

Once the service was over, the couple and their attendants mounted their horses again and rode out of the ceremony area to a clearing outside of the tent. The pictures were taken there.

THE WEDDING FEAST

Instead of a traditional reception, a wedding feast followed the ceremony. According to Mellinda, a medieval wedding feast is a long, joyous affair full of food, music, and merriment. The food comes in a series of courses and is served family style. "Most medieval foods are eaten with one's fingers or with a spoon and a knife. Forks were not common at the time; only the very rich had forks, and generally even then they were not used. Food was eaten off of a wooden trencher or bowl," says Mellinda.

In keeping with the period, each guest had a wooden bowl, a wooden spoon, a bowl of water (to rinse their hands), and a cloth to wipe the mess from their fingers. For those who did not bring their own daggers, knives were provided.

Instead of having separate tables, the couple placed tables together in a U shape under the tent, and the head table formed the bottom of the U. The tables were covered with green and black tablecloths, and the centerpieces were simple green glass vases with candles set in sand.

The food, which came in two courses, included bread, greens, asparagus, carrots, sausages, roast venison and roast beef with spiced blueberry sauce, lamb stew on a bed of smashed potatoes, fresh fruit, cheese, and assorted tortes. It was served on platters that were passed to each guest.

The entertainment between courses was a trunk show—a skit put on by three or four actors with the help of the audience. "There was a great deal of audience participation during the trunk show," says Mellinda. "Our best man, Garry, a six-foot-six guy with a beard, played the part of the beautiful princess. It was a hoot!"

After the trunk show, toasts were offered, the cake was cut, and the bouquet was tossed. Instead of having a garter toss, the couple had a favor toss. "Women did not wear garters at the time, so they took an old coin, wrapped it in a linen hanky, tied it with a ribbon, and had the hubby toss that instead," explains Mellinda.

Near the end of the festivities, a northeaster threatened to blow in. The party wrapped up, and Mellinda and Rondell headed to their getaway car. Despite the iffy weather (thankfully, it didn't rain), the couple had a blast on their wedding day. "It was a great big 'family' party—big enough that most everyone we wanted to be there was there, but small enough [for us] to spend quality time with each guest," says Mellinda.

- If you are planning a wedding with a historical theme, look for modern substitutes to period pieces (e.g., the couple used wooden salad bowls for the wooden trenchers).

- If you want to make your own costumes, plan to have everything done at least one month in advance. Buy or rent anything you don't have made by then.

- Be prepared for naysayers who will tell you that you can't, or shouldn't, do what you want. You can; just figure out how to do it.

Mellinda

Mellinda and Rondell's Wedding Budget

Reception venue, food and beverages	$600
[including cake and service (Amount is for food only; the remainder was free or given as a gift.)]	
Attire	$1,145
Flowers	$40
(Mellinda made her own floral arrangements.)	
Photography	$250
(Amount is for film development only.)	
Stationery	$100
Gifts	$200
Wedding rings	$2,000
Ceremony	$700
[includes location, tables, tents, portable toilets (used for both ceremony and reception)]	
Transportation and parking	$0
Miscellaneous expenses	$250
(including signs to location and assorted decorations)	
Total	**$5,285**

CHAPTER 9

What's Your Destination?

Whether it's on a quiet Hawaiian beach, inside a luxurious Scottish castle, on a shore of a secluded Canadian lake, or in the parlor of a cozy East Coast inn, a destination wedding can be ideal for many reasons.

This chapter explores the advantages of destination weddings and discusses the details of planning a wedding away from home. Finding a location has never been easier. Use the six steps outlined in this chapter to find the perfect location for your big day.

WHY HAVE A DESTINATION WEDDING?

Two of the main reasons that destination weddings have become so popular in recent years are that they are generally (1) less stressful and (2) less expensive than traditional weddings.

By having a destination wedding, a couple can reduce their stress level exponentially—especially if they hire an on-site wedding coordinator to do all the legwork for them. Instead of having to worry about all the wedding-related details—like finding a florist, a photographer, musicians, etc.—a couple can spend time researching their wedding destination for fun things to do there.

If a couple feels pressured to have a large wedding, a destination wedding is a great way to scale things down. Some couples start out planning a traditional wedding at home, but family conflicts over the wedding lead them to opt for a simple wedding away from all the stress at home.

According to Richard Markel, president of the Association for Wedding Professionals International, destination weddings account for approximately 18 percent of all weddings. *(January 2004)*

"My parents are divorced, and we were already dealing with uncomfortable issues and disagreements. It didn't take long before [Michael] and I both agreed a destination wedding would be the answer," says January, who married Michael at a resort in Jamaica.

Even couples who have no conflict with family members over their nuptials enjoy the intimacy that a destination wedding can provide. Having a wedding hundreds or thousands of miles away usually means it will be either just you and your honey or the two of you and a few family members and close friends.

Generally, a destination wedding also means less financial stress—especially if it is combined with the honeymoon, as many are. Numerous hotels and resorts offer all-inclusive "weddingmoon" packages.

Destination weddings are ideal for couples who simply don't have time to plan a wedding at home. Kari and Scott, for instance, got married at an all-inclusive resort in Nassau, Bahamas, because they were both too busy with their careers to plan an at-home wedding. "There was no stress, no worrying about stupid things," says Kari. "We all just had fun."

Another reason destination weddings are all the rage is that, simply put, they're romantic and fun. What better setting to celebrate a major milestone in life than a vacation at a favorite spot? A destination wedding is enjoyable for not only the bride and groom but for their guests—if any are invited.

did _{YOU}
know ?

Destination weddings have
an average of fifty guests.

[source: Washingtonian online
(www.washingtonian.com)]

Couples who want to include guests find that a wedding away is a great opportunity to get everyone together. Many couples have friends and family scattered across the country, and a destination wedding brings everyone together for a good time in the same location. Chances are that guests will attend your wedding and spend time exploring and sight-seeing.

Weddings away are also popular with second-time brides and grooms, many of whom have already done the traditional nuptials. They don't want the hassle of having to plan a wedding at home and would rather have a stress-free celebration.

Paula and Phil, for instance, did not want to plan an elaborate wedding for the second time, so they decided to have a destination wedding in Florida with only eight guests. "I wouldn't trade a single, solitary second of [our] experience," says Paula. She says that when her children are ready to get married, she will encourage them to have destination weddings.

TEN REASONS TO GET MARRIED AWAY

{1} Cheaper

{2} Requires less time to plan

{3} Less stress

{4} More intimate

{5} Fun for the couple and their guests

{6} Adventurous

{7} Unique

{8} Romantic

{9} More spontaneous

{10} Provides opportunity for families to get to know one another

"I Do" in a Scottish Castle

GRISEL AND JEFF weren't planning to marry in a castle in Scotland. In fact, the California couple had made plans to get married on Laguna Beach. They even had the exact spot picked out, but they suddenly got cold feet—not about the marriage, but about the venue. Grisel's listening to her gut paid off. Two weeks before their wedding, the couple read in the local paper that the Laguna Beach company had disappeared, leaving couples who had paid deposits stranded at the last minute.

London, England, was the couple's next choice. However, they discovered they couldn't wed there on their chosen date because they would be required to reside in England for several weeks prior to the wedding.

After learning that Scotland had no such residency requirement, Grisel and Jeff were sold on the location. With the help of a U.K.-based wedding coordinator, they found a castle that seemed ideal for their wedding. Culzean Castle, which was built in the late 1700s on the southwest coast of Scotland in South Ayrshire, is situated on a cliff that provides a dramatic view of the Firth of Clyde and nearby islands.

Besides helping them find the perfect spot, the wedding planner also made arrangements for a photographer, a videographer, a florist, dinner, and accommodations.

Two wedding guests from home and numerous relatives from Scotland attended the evening ceremony, which was held in the castle's salon. "[It's] the most amazing room in the castle with its contrasting traits of eighteenth-century elegance and wild, untamed scenery of sea, sky, and mountain," says Grisel.

After the ceremony and photographs, the couple and their guests enjoyed a specially prepared dinner in the dining room of the castle's Eisenhower Apartment. When the couple arrived home, they held a reception aboard a yacht in Newport Beach, California, for family and friends who were unable to attend the wedding.

Although Grisel wouldn't have changed a thing about the wedding itself, she wishes she had given friends and family more notice so more of them could have attended. "Three months is not enough time. I think six months' notice is the absolute minimum, with a year being ideal," says Grisel.

WHERE TO WED

The biggest decision a couple faces for their destination wedding is where to have it. Some couples might know right away where they want to say their vows: The place is a favorite vacation spot, a place they've always wanted to visit, or a convenient or affordable location. For other couples the choice might not be so easy: The couple agrees on the climate but hasn't made up their minds on the specific place, or worse yet, they prefer places at different ends of the spectrum—Europe for her, the tropics for him.

Some wedding specialists suggest either choosing a location that you have already visited or visiting the location before your wedding to ensure that the place meets your expectations—but that can be expensive. If you have plenty of good information on the location, you've received recommendations from other couples or from travel agents, and you don't mind taking risks, you might want to forgo the visit. If you won't be comfortable making wedding plans without having set foot in the chosen location, visit it first.

SIX STEPS TO CHOOSING A SUITABLE LOCATION

§1§ **Start early**. It's important to nail down a few possibilities early on. Some wedding specialists suggest you start planning six months to one year in advance. The sooner you can start planning your wedding the better. If you plan well in advance, fewer places will be booked up, and you may be able to take advantage of cheaper prices on flights and lodging. Planning ahead will give you more time to research locations. You will also be able to give your guests plenty of notice so they can schedule vacation time and save up for the trip.

§2§ **Learn about the legalities**. Once you have a few possible locations, find out about the marriage laws in each region. France, for instance, has a forty-day residency requirement, whereas Jamaica has only a one-day residency requirement. Several Caribbean islands have residency requirements of one to ten days. If you want to get married in Cancun, you and your sweetie will be required to submit blood tests and copies of your birth certificates or passports.

In the U.S., laws vary from state to state. Hawaii, for example, simply requires driver's licenses. You can get information about what documents and health tests are needed by contacting the county marriage license bureau. Make sure you ask how long paperwork processing takes. Check out www.weddingdetails.com/questions/license.cfm for information on various states.

Many resorts and hotels throughout the world provide wedding coordinators who can help you understand the region's legalities. Some coordinators will even assist you with filing the required paperwork. To get the necessary information on your own, contact the location's tourist office or U.S. consulate or embassy in that country. Some government Web sites and some travel agents are other possible sources of this information. Ask the following questions prior to selecting a location for your wedding.

- What types of documents are needed? Do they have to be translated and/or notarized? Are originals required, or are copies okay?

- What documentation do you need to produce if you are divorced or widowed?

- Is there a residency requirement?

- Are any other waiting periods required?

- Are blood tests or other medical tests required? If so, can your own doctor perform them, or must they be done in the country of marriage?

- How many witnesses are required?

- Are religious wedding ceremonies considered legal, or must they be preceded by a civil ceremony?

§3§ **Find a place that fits your budget**. Your budget will play a role in the location decision. As you figure out how much you want to spend, you'll need to decide whether or not you will pay for your guests' travel expenses. Some couples' wedding budgets allow them to make this nice gesture. Other couples have guests pay their own way, which is also fine. Find out if the hotel or resort offers group rates. Such deals can save you and your guests a chunk of change. If you are on a tight budget, consider a wedding set during the off-season. Choosing a country where the currency exchange rate is favorable can also ease your budget concerns.

CONVERTING YOUR GREENBACKS

Want to find out how your currency fares in other countries? Check out www.xe.com.

§4§ **Find out about wedding packages and wedding coordinators**. If you choose a package deal, make sure you get the lowdown on all the vendors. Look at the photographer's work, and listen to the musicians' demo tape. If a wedding coordinator is included, find out if he will be on-site during your wedding. Having someone on-site to help you with the planning process will make things a lot easier. Many hotels, resorts, and chapels offer wedding planning services.

Whether or not the wedding coordinator's services are part of the package, do your homework. Get the names of some of the coordinator's past clients as references—and check them out. Find out how many out-of-town clients the wedding consultant has had. Check out some online wedding forums where you can talk to other brides about wedding coordinators. Seek advice on whom to consider and whom to avoid.

If you choose to forgo the wedding consultant and plan your own long-distance wedding, find at least one contact who can check out the vendors for you. This can be someone at the destination or a reputable travel agent at home who has plenty of experience with destination weddings.

§5§ **Research the location**. Before you make a final location decision, do plenty of research. Don't choose a place on a whim or just because it seems like a good deal. For each location you seriously consider, find out everything you can, including:

- ꙮ Is the area safe?

- ꙮ Is the water drinkable?

- ꙮ Do you need special vaccinations before arriving?

- ꙮ What's the weather expected to be like around your wedding date? What type of attire will be appropriate?

- ꙮ What types of sight-seeing activities are available?

- ꙮ Are discount rates offered for group tours?

- ꙮ Does the hotel or resort offer activities for children?

- ꙮ How old is the place of lodging?

- ꙮ How many U.S. weddings have been performed at the resort? Are references available to be contacted? Read travel guides, talk to other couples, and check with travel agents who have information on the region.

§6§ **Get it in writing**. Do not rely solely on verbal agreements; get everything in writing! If a vendor doesn't live up to his end of the deal, a hard copy of the agreement will carry a lot more weight than a handshake when you seek your due.

POPULAR DESTINATION LOCATIONS

These are some popular locations for destination weddings. See the Resources section at the back of this book for Web sites on each location.

- ❧ Florida
- ❧ Hawaii
- ❧ Lake Tahoe
- ❧ Las Vegas, Nevada
- ❧ The Bahamas
- ❧ Bermuda

- ❧ British Columbia, Canada
- ❧ Greece
- ❧ Italy
- ❧ Jamaica
- ❧ Mexico
- ❧ Scotland
- ❧ St. Lucia, British West Indies
- ❧ U.S. Virgin Islands

A Destination Wedding for Two, Close to Home

LYNN AND CHARLIE'S wedding on Michigan's Mackinac Island proves that you don't have to leave the country—or even your state—to have the destination wedding of your dreams.

The couple lives near Ann Arbor, Michigan, and had taken numerous trips to Mackinac Island, a popular tourist destination known for its Victorian architecture, beautiful gardens, and quaint shops. The couple felt that it was "one of the most romantic settings on earth" and, therefore, a perfect place for their nuptials.

The couple had been together for fifteen years and wanted to celebrate their wedding with just each other, so no guests were invited. "We wanted it to be a very personal, romantic time without the distractions of having lots of guests. Most of our family and friends had thought of us as a married couple for many, many years anyways, so we didn't need to make a very public statement by the wedding," explains Lynn.

After a short ceremony on the grounds of an inn, the couple took a one-hour carriage ride on the island; their photographer followed them on a bicycle. The ride took them through the town, where tourists lined the streets and shouted their congratulations, and around the countryside.

Later in the day, the couple went by carriage to a local restaurant for dinner and then to the famous Grand Hotel, where they danced their first dance as a married couple. "It was even more wonderful than we dared hope," says Lynn.

YOUR GUESTS

Once you select a location, start letting your loved ones in on the news. Although you'll probably tell those closest to you in person or by phone, you should send all invitees—if you are having any guests—a save-the-date card several months before your wedding.

A save-the-date card is not a formal invitation. It simply tells your guests where and when your upcoming wedding will be held so that they can—you guessed it—save the date well in advance and start saving for the trip! An invitation, with all the specific details, should be sent closer to the big day.

Wedding etiquette says you should send invitations to everyone you want to have at your wedding—regardless of whether you think they'll be able to attend. That way, you reduce the risk of hurt feelings.

DESTINATION WEDDING PRICE TAG

According to a 2003 article on *Time* Online Edition (www.time.com), a destination wedding can cost from $4,000 to $8,000 for ten to twenty people, or $12,000 to $20,000 for fifty guests.

Unless you will pay for your guests' travel, they will need to decide whether they can or want to shell out the money to attend your wedding. Some of your guests will decline your invitation, while others will see it as a wonderful opportunity to take a vacation.

You can help reduce your guests' expenses. One option is to tell them "no gifts, please." Inform your guests of group rates at your wedding venue. Also offer your guests a list of other affordable accommodations.

If your wedding will include no guests or just a handful, send wedding announcements to uninvited friends and family members after the big day. Why not invite them all to a postwedding party? Several couples I interviewed did this. The party can be as casual or as elegant as you like, and it is a great opportunity to share your wedding-day pictures and/or video.

DEALING WITH OPPOSITION

When you tell your loved ones that you will have a destination wedding, their response might be one of surprise, joy, or disappointment.

Cecile and Eugene have family and friends spread across the U.S. and the Philippines. When they revealed that they were getting married at Walt Disney World, their loved ones weren't exactly enthused. "The first time we mentioned Disney to our family and friends they scoffed at us," says Cecile. "Clearly, they all wanted us to get married where they were. Logistically, that would [have been] impossible. . . . [Ultimately] we had to decide what was important to us."

Loved ones who aren't keen on the idea at first might come around. If they don't, they don't. Although you care about your loved ones, it is your wedding. Don't feel guilty about following through with your wedding-day dreams. If you try to please others instead of yourselves, you may look back on your nuptials with regret.

SPENDING TIME WITH YOUR GUESTS

A destination wedding usually makes for an extended celebration. Instead of getting everyone together for just one day, you can spread out the fun over several days.

Several couples I interviewed planned numerous group activities during their wedding stay. They found this to be a great way for the bride's and groom's families to get to know each other better—and it made some wonderful memories.

If you plan an itinerary for your guests, poll them beforehand to find out what types of activities they would enjoy. Make sure the itinerary has some variety and that the activities are affordable for your guests. Let your guests know about the activities well in advance so they have time to decide whether or not they want to participate, and make sure they know that their attendance is optional. Some of your guests might want to hang out by the pool rather than hike through a rain forest.

Don't feel like you have to include everyone in all of your tourist adventures. Sometimes you might want to go it alone or with just your parents or a best friend. Planning a few group activities won't mean that you and your sweetie won't be able to spend most of your time alone. Some couples stay at a different resort than their guests then take off to another location for their honeymoon. How much time you spend with your guests is entirely up to you.

GETTING IT ALL THERE

You've chosen your destination, and the time has arrived to pack your bags. Unlike a typical vacation, you'll have much more to consider than your everyday clothes and toiletries. You'll have to pack everything you will need for your wedding day.

The two of you probably won't be able to just relax and take in all the sights—not right away, that is. When you arrive, contact your wedding coordinator or the vendors to make sure everything is set for your big day.

WHAT ABOUT THE DRESS?

For some items, such as a wedding gown, you'll have to figure out the best way to transport them. You have several options. Most airplanes have cabin closets that can hold a wedding dress during a flight. Contact your airline about this ahead of time, then make sure the dress is packaged properly for the flight and doesn't exceed the size restrictions.

Another option is to check the gown or other item with your luggage. If you're worried

In the rush to pack

for your wedding,

here are a few items you

shouldn't forget:

- ✿ Wedding attire

- ✿ Wedding rings

- ✿ Driver's licenses or
  photo IDs

- ✿ Wedding documents,
  including vendor
  contact information
  and agreements, and
  passports

- ✿ Medical insurance
  information

- ✿ Any medication(s)

- ✿ Foreign currency,
  if needed

about it getting lost—a legitimate concern—don't choose this option. (Our luggage was lost during our honeymoon flight. Thankfully it showed up just a day later.)

Sara and Peter, who got married in Greece, took the chance and checked their wedding-day garb with their baggage. "Our whole getup (my dress, shoes, veil, etc., and Peter's suit) had its own suitcase: a red fold-up garment bag with wheels that we checked through," says Sara. They carried the rest of their bags aboard and placed them in overhead compartments. "It worked out very well," says Sara.

You can also have a service such as UPS or Federal Express ship the dress to your resort or to your wedding coordinator ahead of time. Make arrangements with your wedding coordinator or the hotel concierge to have the dress steamed before the big day.

The groom's attire can be packed along with the wedding dress, as Sara and Peter did. If a tux will be rented at home, ask relatives or friends who will get back before you will to return it. Renting a tux at your destination might be a better option.

THE PLANE HAS LANDED

You finally arrive at your destination. You pick up your luggage—it will *not* get lost—get into your rental car, and head toward your hotel. Once there you find your room—it's lovely—and plunk down on the bed, and breathe a big sigh of relief.

Don't get too comfy just yet. You have a whole day of appointments ahead of you. You should meet with your wedding coordinator (if you have one), your officiant, and the vendors before your wedding.

If your wedding is the day after your arrival, you might be pressed for time. However, if you scheduled a rehearsal, you should be able to meet with the wedding consultant, the officiant, and perhaps a few vendors at that time. If your vendors can't make it, schedule other appointments or at least contact them by phone.

ADDING CULTURAL TOUCHES

Including local touches in your wedding can make your wedding unique and memorable. Food, music, and costumes from the region can add flare to your wedding.

You can also incorporate the culture's traditional wedding customs into your nuptials.

If you get married in Hawaii, you could both wear flower leis and have Hawaiian musicians play the "Hawaiian Wedding Song" on instruments such as a ukulele or steel guitar. Would the groom be up for arriving in a canoe? Food for the reception could include sweet-and-sour pineapple shrimp, crab cakes, and a variety of tropical fruit.

If Italy's your destination, give your guests sugared almonds, which symbolize both the bitter and the sweet aspects of marriage. Indulge in an Italian feast of calamari, bruschetta, pasta, and Italian wine. Serve tiramisu for dessert.

Getting married in Bermuda? Plant a tree on your wedding day to symbolize the growth of your love. Some couples use a sapling as the wedding cake topper then plant the tree during the reception.

To get ideas for your wedding, research your chosen location at the library or on the Internet. Also consult your wedding coordinator, officiant, or other on-site contact.

WEDDINGS AT DISNEY

Walt Disney World in Orlando, Florida, offers a bunch of options when it comes to weddings. You can have one or several Disney characters play a role in your wedding. If you want to feel like Cinderella, you can rent her crystal coach.

A Wedding Under the Jamaican Sun

JANUARY AND MICHAEL were warm and toasty at their Jamaica wedding while chilly March winds blew back home. They reside in Ohio and wanted to escape the stress and hassle of planning a wedding at home. The two of them chose a destination wedding at the Renaissance Jamaica Grande Resort in Ocho Rios, Jamaica.

For weddings, Jamaica has a residency requirement of only one day. "We chose Jamaica for the ease of getting married," says January, adding that the resort took care of all the paperwork for them through the mail before they left for Jamaica. A local travel agent recommended the resort, and the resort provided the couple with an on-site wedding planner who arranged everything from photography to flowers.

Although the couple initially thought about going alone, they were glad they invited their twenty-three guests. This included three nieces and nephews who were under age nine and were easily occupied at the pool and the beach. "We decided to throw it out there and let anyone who wanted to come along. In the end we were glad we had friends and family there to share it all with," says January.

The "short but meaningful" ceremony, complete with tropical breezes and exotic flowers, was held near the ocean. A reception followed on a patio along the beach. The couple and their guests enjoyed dinner, cake, and champagne. After dinner, they all attended a beach party hosted by the hotel.

The day after the wedding, the couple headed to a resort in Negril for their honeymoon. When the couple returned home, a wedding shower and a small reception were held, allowing the couple to show the wedding pictures and video to people who could not attend the wedding.

WHERE TO RESEARCH ONLINE

Because of the increasing popularity of destination weddings, a slew of Web sites are devoted to the topic. Whether you're looking for marriage laws for a particular region or details of wedding packages, you'll find that the Internet is a great resource. Here are just a few examples. More Web sites are listed in the Resources section at the back of this book.

- ☙ **www.destinationbride.com.** This helpful resource provides information on destination weddings around the world.

- ☙ **www.weddingsabroad.com.** This site offers planning services for weddings throughout the world. It includes articles, a discussion forum, feature weddings, information on legal requirements, and a destination directory.

- ☙ **www.whollymatrimony.com/Webrings/destination.html**. This site has a wide variety of information on destination weddings, including couple profiles, a discussion forum, articles on planning, and FAQs (frequently asked questions) on destination weddings. It also offers links to other Web sites.

- ☙ **www.personal.umich.edu/~kzaruba/wedding.html**. Tips on planning a destination wedding and links galore can be found at this Web site.

Several online message boards are devoted to the topic of destination weddings. If you have a question or would simply like to read about other couples' experiences, check out the discussion boards at www.blissweddings.com and www.talkaboutweddings.com.

A Wedding in Greece

SARA & PETER

SANTORINI, GREECE

THE MEETING:	"Mutual friends were dating through personals; we were chaperoning our friends. They didn't stay together, but we did!" says Sara.
THE PROPOSAL:	Sara and Peter had lived together for two years and were both absorbed in their careers. In fact, they had been putting off marriage because of their hectic work lives. Finally, one night, Peter proposed. "Peter woke me up around 11:30 P.M. by slipping an engagement ring [on my finger] and asking me to marry him. Half asleep I muttered 'yes,' kissed him, and rolled over and went back to sleep," says Sara.
CEREMONY:	Hotel Esperas, Oia, Santorini, Greece
RECEPTION:	Restaurant 1800
NUMBER OF GUESTS:	13
COST:	$10,350; paid for by the bride and groom. (This amount includes the honeymoon. Family members paid for their own travel and lodging.)
PLANNING DURATION:	5 months

Although Sara and Peter had never been to Greece, they had seen enough photographs of the country to know that it would be a gorgeous setting for their nuptials.

After checking several Web sites, they fell in love with the island of Santorini and the village of Oia. Perched high atop a cliff overlooking the sea, Oia is considered one of the most picturesque villages in Santorini. "The same day as our ceremony, the Victoria's Secret crew was shooting their catalog two hotels up from ours. That's how beautiful the location is," says Sara.

PLANNING

Sara and Peter, who reside in Pacific Palisades, California, knew from the moment they got engaged that they didn't want a big, conventional wedding. "I believe that most weddings are ... outrageously frivolous and expensive," says Sara. She also has no use for many of the typical wedding-day traditions. "The traditions of weddings are outdated, ... and the concepts did not suit us in our lives."

With their families spread around the world, Sara and Peter thought a destination wedding would not only be perfect for the two of them but also a great way to get their loved ones together for a vacation. "We [had] never taken a family vacation together and thought it would be fun to remove everybody from their element, go to some magical location, and have the ceremony without the drama," says Sara.

They didn't "officially" invite anyone. In fact, not one formal invitation was sent. "I called my immediate family ... to see who could possibly come but explained that they should not attend if traveling to Greece would either be a financial or time strain. ... Our friends were notified either by e-mail or casual phone conversation," says Sara. "We presented the wedding as an elopement and [that] if they wanted to attend, this is when and where it would be."

Presenting their nuptials this way made it easier for the couple to deal with family squabbles over the wedding. "When parents started the typical prewedding disagreements, we always answered that if they did not approve of our choices, they should not feel pressured to attend. This always ended arguments abruptly," says Sara.

STRESS FREE

Sara and Peter say planning their wedding was virtually stress free, and much of that had to do with the fact that they hired an on-site wedding coordinator who had been recommended by a friend of the family. The wedding coordinator offered a complete wedding package, including airfare and hotel. However, the couple had already booked the flight and accommodations, as well as the photographer, so the wedding coordinator just arranged everything else. "[He] handled the legal paperwork, legal translation, ceremony, musicians, flowers, donkeys, hairdressers, fireworks, balloons, reception, and cake for a package price," says Sara.

HAVING AN OPEN MIND

According to Sara, Greeks have a different philosophy on wedding planning than that of Americans. "The Greeks are very laid back about planning a wedding, ... and they believe it will all work out in the end, which it usually does," Sara says. "In America, it seems like part of our tradition is for the bride to become obsessed with every detail."

Sara has spoken with many other brides who have had destination weddings, and she's come to the conclusion that Greeks aren't the only ones who have a different take on weddings. "Culturally there can be big differences [in] how weddings are organized.... That can be the exciting and unique part of the wedding, or it can drive people crazy to not have things exactly as they have planned them," she says. Sara got more out of the experience by having an open mind. "Sometimes you need to tone [down] your desire for control ... or else the fun will be taken out of the experience."

THE MAIN EVENT

The couple was married poolside at sunset. The ceremony started with three of Peter's cousins, ages five to eight, throwing rose petals on the pool deck while musicians played traditional Greek music for guests seated beside the pool.

After saying their vows, the couple released balloons, which is a typical Greek tradition. Then, fireworks in hand, the couple walked uphill to their "Greek limo," a white donkey for the bride and a brown donkey for the groom.

Sara wasn't exactly keen on the idea of riding a donkey through town, but her new husband convinced her to hop aboard. "Peter quickly made up a story and said 'It's a Greek custom. You'll insult them if you don't ride the donkey through town.' So I dutifully jumped onto the donkey, and off we went," explains Sara. She had no regrets. In fact, she said that for the fifteen minutes it took to get to the reception site, she felt like a rock star. "It's difficult to explain how thrilling and exciting it was to ride throughout the town while the local townspeople and tourists alike cheered, clapped, and took pictures. There were hundreds of tourists who all came out to see this parade through town. It was like we were the entertainment for the city that night," says Sara.

The couple dismounted from their donkeys in front of a five-star restaurant, where they and their guests enjoyed a modern Greek gourmet dinner. "The food was awesome," says Sara.

The following day the couple held an appreciation dinner for their guests. The day after that, the couple went to the island of Crete for a five-day honeymoon. "Some of the family stayed in Santorini, some of them went to Athens, and some [went] to Paris," says Sara.

TIME WITH LOVED ONES

The couple planned numerous activities in Greece, with their guests. They hiked to the top of a volcano, took a trip to a local winery, visited a local town, and toured an archeological site.

For those who couldn't make it to the wedding, Peter's mother hosted a party at a Greek restaurant three weeks after the couple arrived home. "She was able to invite all her friends that would have attended a traditional wedding if we had had one. I also was able to invite our friends that were not able to attend the original Greek shindig," says Sara.

HAPPY ENDING

Although their families weren't too enthused with the idea of their destination wedding at first, Sara and Peter are glad they persevered—and they're grateful that loved ones were there for their special day. "It cost the same amount as a typical honeymoon, and we got to travel to a fantastic place with our families," says Sara.

BRIDE TO BRIDE

· Get plenty of information on the location you consider. Hotel Esperas had 360-degree video of the entire hotel, so we knew exactly what we were getting, and so did our guests.

· Don't try to coordinate your guests' travel; that's too much to handle.

· Hire someone, such as a wedding coordinator, at the location to handle all of the details.

· Think about currency exchange. You can either get a great deal or pay way more depending on the country and the exchange rate.

· Get rid of your traditional wedding expectations and go with the flow. What you wind up with will be better than what your controlling imagination will allow. For example, how many people can say they rode to the reception on a donkey!

Sara

Sara and Peter's Wedding & Honeymoon Budget

Reception venue, food, and beverages *(including cake and service)*	$1,000
Attire	$1,800
Photography/videography	$300
Stationery	$0
Gifts	$250
Wedding rings	$1,000
Wedding coordinator's wedding package	$2,000
Travel *(including accommodations, airfare, etc.)*	$4,000
Total	**$10,350**

CHAPTER 10

Tying the Knot . . . Again

Encore brides and grooms generally have a different approach to weddings than they did when they married the first time. Many of them have different priorities (e.g., careers, kids, homes), and they no longer feel pressured by their families or society to have a traditional wedding. Today's encore brides and grooms have the freedom to create a wedding that suits their own personal tastes—whether that means a lavish wedding with no expense spared or a simple "I do" with no guests.

This chapter also discusses reaffirmations. With wedding renewals becoming more popular, intimate ceremonies are playing a role in re-affirming a couple's love and commitment to each other.

Paula and Phil had both been married before. This time around, they wanted an intimate, stress-free wedding on the beach rather than a big, white, conventional wedding. "I wanted my wedding to Phil to be something between the two of us, not [an event] to cater to everyone else's needs and desires. Been there, done that!" says Paula.

Some brides and grooms go all out on their second wedding, especially if they didn't have the wedding they wanted the first time. Perhaps the first wedding was simple when they wanted something lavish. Conversely, maybe the first time around they opted for the puffy white dress with sequins, the tux with tails, fourteen attendants, the stretch limo, and a three-tier wedding cake when they wanted one with an emphasis on fun rather than formality.

Either way, couples tying the knot for the second time seem to have a lot more freedom to do as they please. The only hard-and-fast rule seems to be that the second-time bride should not wear a blusher veil, which symbolizes virginity.

Gone are the days when a second-time bride can't wear white. Gone are the days when second weddings aren't as bold and magnificent as any other major celebration. If you're planning a second wedding, keep your mind open to all of the possibilities. Maybe a destination wedding to your favorite out-of-the-way haunt will be perfect for you, or maybe the park just around the corner from home would suit you better. Perhaps a wedding at your home would be ideal. Or maybe Las Vegas is calling.

A Wedding in the Stratosphere

MICHELE AND ERIC had both been married before and done the large traditional wedding; the kind that "stays within the lines" and where the families call the shots. This time, they wanted a celebration that was entirely different.

Living in Las Vegas, the couple didn't have to go far to have a wedding that was fun and laid back. In the Stratosphere Hotel Casino and Tower 103 floors above the Las Vegas skyline, the couple wed—surrounded by sixty-four guests. The ceremony was performed by a nonsectarian minister and took place just after sundown. "There were windows around three-quarters of the chapel. What a great view!" says Michele.

Instead of having a loved one walk her down the aisle, Michele chose to go it alone. "My mom walked [with] me the first time, and I was going to ask her again . . . but I am a believer in signs and karma, and I honestly didn't want this second (and last!) wedding to resemble the first in any way," says Michele.

Neither Michele nor Eric had children at the time. In fact, no children at all were involved in the wedding. "At my first wedding I had a flower girl [who] was way too young (just over a year old) just to [be able to] say I had a flower girl. This time I didn't have one or want one," says Michele.

After the ceremony the couple and their guests went up one floor to a banquet room for a sit-down dinner of filet mignon and salmon. "Eric and I hate to dance, so we didn't have dancing, and you know what? No one cared," says Michele. "We did have music . . . that allowed us to actually communicate with our guests [without] shouting."

Michele, whose first wedding was held in a catering hall with one hundred guests, says that she and Eric were very selective when choosing their guests. "There wasn't one person there that we didn't know. Everyone there was very special to us in some way. That was not true [my] first time," says Michele.

Overall, Michele's perspective on weddings changed greatly since her first wedding. "It definitely makes me smile and shake my head when I see brides-to-be obsessing about all these details that are, in hindsight, so unimportant."

WHAT'S THIS ABOUT WEARING WHITE?

Although most brides tend to tone things down a bit for a second wedding, plenty of these brides still wear a white wedding dress. While the dress doesn't usually have beads, sequins, or a four-foot train, it can still be elegant.

Michele chose to wear a white wedding dress, but she had the back lowered six inches and had the train shortened to make it more non-traditional. "This time I got the dress that I wanted and that reflected my style, not the dress that made my mom cry," she says. She did not wear a veil.

Whether a second-time bride opts for a wedding dress in white or her favorite color, she generally chooses a simpler design—and she doesn't have to mind looking sexy. In fact, more and more second-time brides choose body-hugging designs with cutouts that show off some skin.

A sleek, sexy dress is far from being the only choice. Second-time brides can get away with wearing anything from pantsuits to floral sundresses.

YOU ARE NOT ALONE

If you are an encore bride you have lots of company: Of the 2.4 million marriages each year in the U.S., 43 percent are remarriages.

[source: The Orange County Register www.azcentral.com/weddings)]

WHAT'S ON TOP?

When it comes to headgear, wedding etiquette says a blusher veil is definitely out for any wedding after the first one. However, other options such as off-the-face veils, tiaras, hats, bun rings, and flowers are fine. A second-time bride also has the option of wearing nothing at all—on her head, that is.

OUTFITTING THE GROOM

Depending on the style of the wedding, a second-time groom might wear a bowler hat and tails or a Hawaiian shirt and shorts. Like the second-time bride, he is free to wear whatever he deems appropriate. For an outdoor garden wedding, he might wear a light-colored suit or simply dress pants and a dress shirt without a tie. For a formal indoor wedding, he might opt for a black tux.

WHAT ABOUT GIFTS?

Repeat brides and grooms still have opportunities to receive gifts. According to wedding etiquette, it's perfectly acceptable to have a bridal shower for a remarriage. Although guests might give you gifts on your wedding day, experts say that you should not expect wedding presents. (They also say that you shouldn't *expect* gifts at a first wedding either.)

If your wedding is not your first, you probably already have plenty of household items. Consider using a gift registry so that your guests will know exactly what you need. (See chapter two for registry alternatives such as a honeymoon registry or a charity registry.)

Some couples do not want presents from their guests. Michele and Eric, for instance, said "Your presence is our present" on their invitations so their guests would not feel obligated to bring gifts.

MORE TIPS FOR PLANNING A SECOND WEDDING

On average, a second-time wedding has between seventy-five and one hundred guests.

[source: The Orange County Register

www.azcentral.com/weddings)]

- If you are divorced and want to have a church wedding, check with the cleric well before the big day to make sure the church permits second weddings; some faiths do not. If you get turned away, try other churches or seek a nondenominational minister or a justice of the peace.

- Find out if the church requires counseling prior to the wedding.

- If you will pay for your own wedding, word your invitations accordingly. For example: "Cindy Smith and Mike Jones invite you to celebrate with them as they unite in marriage." Invitations can be formal or informal. It's also perfectly okay to call everyone instead of sending a printed invitation.

- Instead of being "given away," have your dad, mom, daughter, groom, or any other special someone escort you down the aisle. It's also perfectly acceptable to go it alone.

A Yacht Wedding

BECKY AND BRYAN, when both were in their early thirties, celebrated their nuptials aboard a yacht in Newport Beach, California. "We didn't want the typical hotel ballroom setting for our reception, as we are both pretty casual people," says Becky.

This wedding was much different than Becky's first wedding. "My first wedding was in Las Vegas. We eloped," she says. "I got married for the first time when I was twenty-one years old. . . . Being young and naive, I married for all the wrong reasons. Now I am married to the man I love for all the right reasons, and we wanted to be able to share our special day with the ones we love as well," she says.

Becky and Bryan chose a small wedding not only because it meant they could spend quality time with their guests but also because it fit with Becky's comfort zone. "I was kind of freaked out about two hundred people staring at me for an entire day. I know it sounds silly, but that is the truth," she says.

Unlike her first wedding, this time Becky had children to consider—a twelve-year old son from her first marriage and a two-year-old daughter with her new groom. Her son acted as a groomsman, even though that idea didn't exactly thrill him at first. "The hardest part for me was that my son kept saying he didn't want to go to the wedding because it would be 'dumb and boring,' but once he got to put on that tuxedo he felt special and thought he looked like James Bond!" says Becky.

After a morning ceremony on the beach, the couple and their forty-five guests boarded the Mojo Yacht for a four-hour luncheon reception that had a beach theme. They enjoyed a meal followed by music and dancing. A couple of hours into the reception, guests mingled on the bow of the boat in the gorgeous weather.

Although Becky admits that planning this wedding was more stressful than her elopement to Las Vegas, she has no regrets. "I told [Bryan] when we got engaged that I wanted a real wedding that included a gown and all that comes with it. A few months into the planning, I was overwhelmed with all that was involved . . . but I am so glad we had the 'real' wedding I always wanted," she says. "It was a big hit, and everyone enjoyed the day."

INVOLVING CHILDREN

If you or your fiancé has kids, you need to consider how they will fit into your wedding-day plans. Getting them involved is a great way to prevent them from feeling alienated and to help them get excited about your "I dos."

Before you make any assumptions about the kids' participation, ask them how they feel about playing a role. Some kids won't be interested. Others might want to work behind the scenes. Still others might want to share the spotlight. Give your child some options, and let him choose a role that suits him.

HELPING PREPARE FOR THE BIG DAY

Encouraging kids to offer input on wedding-day decisions will make them feel like part of things. Let them make suggestions on everything from music to favors. A daughter might want to help pick out the bride's dress. A son might help the groom choose his wedding attire.

Kids who are into crafts might enjoy helping make the invitations, wedding programs, and place cards, as well as wrapping favors. Older children might enjoy helping decorate the venue for the occasion.

Terry got plenty of help for her wedding from her daughter, who also served as the maid of honor. "My daughter helped a lot. . . . We made the invitations, response cards, and many other items ourselves," she says.

CEREMONIAL ROLES

A girl under ten years old might get a kick out of being a flower girl or a ring bearer. A boy that young could serve as a ring bearer.

Paula had her four-year-old son act as the ring bearer for her destination wedding at a beach. "He held the ring box in his hands and wore a beaming smile on his beautiful face as he walked up to Phil and extended his hand. This was my first cause for [a] tissue. At that moment I couldn't have been more proud of my little man!" says Paula.

Preteens could serve as junior bridesmaids or junior ushers. A teenager or adult could serve as a bridesmaid, groomsman, usher, maid of honor, or best man. A special activity for a child of any age is to escort the bride (or groom) down the aisle.

READINGS, SPEECHES, AND MUSIC

Some children might loathe the idea of having to read a passage or a poem at a wedding. Let them choose a role that is more comfortable for them—otherwise, they'll dread the wedding. Kids who don't mind public speaking could participate by doing a biblical reading, reciting a poem, or even giving a speech that she wrote for the occasion. Kids who are musically gifted may want to perform during the ceremony.

VOWS AND THE FAMILY MEDALLION CEREMONY

Many second-time brides and grooms write their own vows, often they include the children. The couple professes their love and devotion to each other and to the children.

The kids can be part of a unity candle ceremony by joining the couple to light the unity candle. Another way to include kids in the ceremony is to have a family medallion ceremony, which can be incorporated into services of all faiths and into civil ceremonies, as well. After the couple exchanges rings, their children join them at the altar. Each child is given a medallion with three intertwining circles that symbolize family love.

Terry and Shannon, who had a Renaissance-themed wedding, had a family medallion ceremony that involved Terry's daughter. "Shannon took a paper out of his pocket, and his best man handed him the family medallion necklace. . . . Shannon put it on Nici, reading his vows to her to "cherish, care for, and support her; to make the house we lived in a home filled with love, laughter, and respect," says Terry. "The judge then bound our three hands with a braided silken ribbon to symbolize our new family unity and announced us to the guests as a family bonded." Terry says that, for her, the family medallion ceremony was the highlight of the wedding.

KIDS AND THE RECEPTION

The ceremony is over and the pictures have been taken. Now it's time to celebrate. Although you and your new spouse might be excited to kick back and have some fun, your kids might be getting antsy—especially if they are wee ones.

Consider making prior arrangements with a relative or friend to keep an eye on the kids during your wedding day. That way you can rest assured that the kids are not unattended while you perform your wedding duties.

Inviting other children to the wedding can help keep your kids occupied. Some couples go as far as hiring clowns, magicians, and other entertainers for the kids. Some children, on the other hand, will relish all the excitement of a wedding. They won't need extra entertainment or baby-sitters. They'll simply have a good time on their own. If that's the case, relax and enjoy!

HONEYMOONING WITH KIDS

Following a second wedding, many couples forget the romantic getaway for two and take a vacation with the kids. For couples who choose a destination wedding, a "familymoon" is common. In fact, many resorts now offer "familymoon" packages that include family activities. Some even include baby-sitting services so couples can have some time alone.

The **Westin St. John Resort and Villas** in the U.S. Virgin Islands offers a family vacation package designed especially for remarrying couples with kids. The package includes two rooms (one for the newlyweds, one for the children), a wedding ceremony with all the trimmings, and an evening for two children at the Westin Kids Club.

Not all remarrying couples want to spend their honeymoon with their kids. Some want the jacuzzi, the privacy, and the champagne for two on the terrace. Some of these couples simply take off for their honeymoon after explaining to their kids that they'd like some time alone.

Other couples plan a honeymoon for just the two of them and a vacation with their children—a great way to please everyone!

RESEARCHING SECOND WEDDINGS

Not surprisingly, the Internet is an invaluable resource for planning a second wedding. Sites discuss everything from etiquette to fashion to great places to tie the knot for a second time. Here are a couple of examples:

- ❧ www.brideagain.com. *Bride Again* is an online magazine that discusses a variety of issues regarding second weddings. Articles include "Designing Your Own Wedding Ring," "Honeymoon Hideaways in Cancun," and "Coping With His Ex."

- ❧ www.gettingremarried.com. This informative Web site discusses everything from invitation wording to financial planning. This site addresses legality issues of second marriages and has a message board.

REAFFIRMATIONS

You've tied the knot and decided that on your first anniversary you want to renew your vows and remind each other of your mutual commitment. Such reaffirmations can be part of any wedding anniversary. Couples don't have to wait until they are old and gray.

While some couples completely re-create the wedding day—complete with the original wedding attire and a reception—others choose to simply recite their vows in a quiet setting by themselves. Just like for your wedding, you get to decide how simple or lavish you want your vow renewal to be. Ultimately, what's important is the celebration that the love between the two of you is still thriving.

Gayle and John decided to have a private wedding renewal at Graceland Chapel in Las

Vegas to celebrate their second anniversary. The renewal service had traditional elements that their California beach wedding did not have. "Our wedding had some wonderful elements, truly wonderful and once-in-a-lifetime, full-of-meaning type stuff . . . but in that, we created a wedding vision which was also extremely nontraditional. I was proud of its uniqueness, but somehow, as the years progressed, I found myself hungering for a wee bit of tradition—and I wanted to feel and look really bridal," explains Gayle. "The renewal gave me that wonderful little piece of the wedding puzzle that I had missed and realized I longed for."

Gayle says that the renewal was stress free, and she recommends this type of service to other couples celebrating an anniversary. "I am so incredibly glad we did it. . . . Along with [our] wedding, [it] will be fondly remembered as one of the most magical days of my life!" she says.

If you plan on a vow renewal service, keep the following questions in mind:

- What location will be suitable? Will you use the same place or choose another romantic destination?

- Do you want to say the vows you recited on your wedding day or create new ones?

- Will a clergyman conduct the service?

- Will you invite guests? If so, will you send printed invitations?

- Will you have music?

- Will you include your children? If so, how?

Whether it's an informal gathering or an elegant celebration, a renewal service can be the ideal way to reflect on the love you share with your spouse and the commitment you've made to each other. Just like your wedding, your renewal celebration will make for special memories to cherish in the years to come.

© 2002 D W PENA

A Second Wedding
in Yosemite National Park

~

ELLEN & TONY

YOSEMITE NATIONAL PARK, CALIFORNIA

THE MEETING:	The couple met during the Alaska AIDS Vaccine Ride in August 2001. They were both crew captains on the fund-raising bike ride. "At the closing ceremonies, I caught him staring at me from across the crowd. Afterwards, he came over and helped me with my gear. I thought I'd never see him again, since I live in California and he was in Minnesota. However, a few days after I got home, I received an e-mail from him. I answered, and things got started from there," says Ellen.
THE PROPOSAL:	Tony wouldn't move from Minnesota to California to be with Ellen and her son unless there was a marriage plan. He proposed to Ellen on New Year's Day in 2002.
CEREMONY:	Glacier Point, Yosemite National Park
RECEPTION:	Picnic area in Yosemite National Park's valley floor
NUMBER OF GUESTS:	36
COST:	$6,125; paid for by the bride and groom
PLANNING DURATION:	5 months

The first time Ellen married, she had a large, traditional church wedding that conformed to guidebook wedding etiquette. "My first wedding hadn't the slightest trace of originality. I was in my mid-twenties, and it never even occurred to me that my wedding could be, or should be, any different than any of the weddings of my friends," explains Ellen. When it came to planning her first wedding, Ellen didn't even have much input. The fact that she was living in Japan at the time made planning a wedding in California difficult. "I chose my dress and the processional music. Mom did the rest," says Ellen.

Ellen and Tony, who reside in Sacramento, California, wanted a wedding that reflected their personalities and unconventional tastes and that emphasized the sacredness of their vows. Both were active in the planning process and devoted a great deal of time to discussing how to make the ceremony meaningful. "We have both attended lots of weddings over the years and felt that the sacredness of the marriage ceremony often gets lost in the hoopla that comes with a large event," says Ellen.

THE CEREMONY

When trying to decide on a wedding location, Tony asked Ellen to fantasize about her dream wedding—the kind she would choose if money were no object. The Yosemite National Park idea grew from there. "I was very excited about sharing a place I love with people we love," says Ellen. The couple chose Glacier Point, thirty-two hundred feet above the Yosemite Valley, as the place for their vows. The location allows stunning views of forests, meadows, cliffs, and distant wilderness areas within the park.

In keeping with his Scottish ancestry, Tony and his best man wore kilts. Ellen, on the other hand, wore a traditional white wedding dress but opted for a hat instead of a veil or tiara. The couple chose one attendant each. Tony's best man was his best friend, and Ellen's was her eleven-year-old son.

Involving Ellen's son in all aspects of the wedding was of utmost importance to the couple. "Tony and I wanted to involve Gregory in such a way that he would understand that we were building a family and that his participation and approval were crucial," says Ellen.

The fifteen-minute ceremony was held at 1 P.M. in a tiny amphitheater carved out of rock and overlooking the valley. "It was a sunny, cloudless day with views for about seventy-five miles," says Ellen. The ceremony began with a bagpiper, who called people to their seats with some traditional Scottish tunes, and was officiated by a friend.

To make the event even more meaningful, the couple wrote the vows themselves. "My husband is not a Christian and I am, so much thought went into demonstrating respect to our beliefs. Tony researched Celtic and pagan wedding ceremonies on the Internet, and we rewrote madly," explains Ellen. The two were also adamant about including Ellen's son in their vows.

THE RECEPTION

A picnic luncheon on the park's valley floor followed the ceremony. The couple hired a caterer from a nearby town to provide the meal. "She hauled in tables, chairs, linens, and china and transformed the grove," says Ellen.

Guests, who had been encouraged to dress for comfort and fun, enjoyed the meal and made the most of their surroundings. "We have some terrific pictures of guests wading in the river!" says Ellen. The reception included no bouquet toss, garter toss, or dancing, but people made toasts. Much to her delight, Ellen's son had prepared a surprise toast for the occasion. "Unbeknownst to anyone, he'd written and memorized a speech, and [he] delivered it as if he spoke publicly every day of his life. Everyone was in tears. I was speechless," says Ellen. She had initially had to beg her son to be her best man, and she had promised him that he wouldn't have to speak or do anything. His speech is her most treasured memory of the day. "I was deeply moved by his words," says Ellen.

BRIDE TO BRIDE

- Try not to revisit your first wedding memories or compare the two events. That can dim the excitement for your fiancé.

- Don't be afraid to ask your family and friends about their interest in the event. We nearly didn't choose Yosemite because we assumed that our family and friends wouldn't be interested in making that kind of journey. Instead, they shared our excitement and made several suggestions that really enhanced the wedding.

- If children are involved, consider their feelings about the changes to their life and keep the lines of communication open.

Ellen

Ellen and Tony's Wedding Budget

Reception venue, music, food, and beverages *(including cake and service)*	$1,750
Attire	$525
Flowers	$100
Photography/videography *(This was a gift from a co-worker.)*	$0
Stationery	$150
Gifts	$250
Wedding rings	$3,200
Ceremony	$150
Total	**$6,125**

CHAPTER 11

Keeping the Memories Alive

In the years since my wedding, I have continued to bask in the sweet memories of that joyful day like a cozy cat on a sunny windowsill. I recall specific moments and feel amazed at how wonderfully it all worked out. I think about my ninety-six-year-old grandmother being there, looking so lovely with her pink suit and her freshly curled silver hair. Sixteen months after the wedding, she passed away. As I look at her image in wedding pictures, I feel both joy and sadness but mainly gratefulness. I am grateful to have had her there, alongside other loved ones who have made a difference in my life.

Your wedding day comes and goes so quickly, so this chapter is dedicated to exploring the ways to keep the memories with you for a lifetime.

PHOTOGRAPHS TO HAVE AND TO HOLD

Of the many ways to keep your wedding memories alive, wedding photographs are one of the best. A single wedding photo can bring back a deluge of memories. Photographs make your memories tangible—frozen in time—and can last for generations. An album full of mediocre snapshots does a disservice to your special day. Although you might look at your wedding pictures only once a year, those photographs should bring back your wedding moments in all of their glory. The photos should make you feel like you are back there.

PHOTO PROTECTION

If you decide to frame your wedding photos, make sure you use acid-free mats. Over time, acid will cause photos to deteriorate.

Photographs provide a great way for you and your spouse to reflect together on your marriage. January and Michael, for instance, look at their wedding album together on each wedding anniversary.

Other couples have their photographs on display instead of tucked away in an album. Ellen and Tony, for instance, created what they call the "wedding wall." "We had eleven of our favorite photos enlarged to different sizes and then put them into coordinating frames. Some are displayed on top of the dresser, and the rest [are] arranged on the wall behind [it]," Ellen says.

Christina and Neal made an "art gallery" out of their wedding photographs. "We have a photo album, but unlike a traditional one, we customized it into a glass art box where each individual photo is matted. Every month we . . . randomly select a few prints and hang them up to create our own little gallery," explains Christina.

Another display option for your wedding photos is a photomontage, a collage of photos placed together to form a larger image. You can make one yourself or have one professionally made.

WEDDING MUSIC

If you make a Web site or a CD to display your favorite wedding photos, why not burn a CD of your wedding-day music? Every time you play the CD you will return to that special event in your life.

GOING DIGITAL

More and more couples are using the computer to display their wedding photos. Some store their photos on a CD, making a digital photo album that can be viewed on the computer. Others create their own Web sites to display their pictures or transfer their photos to other Web sites that display wedding photos.

Melanie and Rod, for instance, uploaded their wedding photos to Ofoto (www.ofoto.com) for easy viewing by faraway friends and family. This gives them online storage of their photos. "[We have] the peace of mind [of knowing] that if we lose the pictures, they will always be online," says Melanie.

Mellinda and Rondell created a Web page (www.geocities.com/sideseat/weddinghome.html) to highlight their medieval-themed wedding. Mellinda admits it's not as permanent as a scrapbook, but she says the Web site has been a great way to keep track of things and to share the wedding with others. "When we are asked about the wedding, we can just send people to the site. It allows us to share our experiences with a lot of different people as well as our extended family members who live far away," she says. She even gets at least two e-mails a month from strangers inquiring about the medieval-themed wedding.

Sara, who designs Web sites for a living, created a personal wedding Web site at www.idomemories.com. It includes hundreds of pictures of Sara and Peter's destination wedding in Greece. "We had so many photos [almost five hundred] that it was much simpler to create a Web site with many different sections that could hold an infinite amount of pictures," Sara says. The majority of their photos were taken with a digital camera, so they actually look better on the computer than in hard copy.

Aside from having instant access to their wedding day memories, the Web site has also made it easier for Sara and Peter's friends and family to enjoy the photos. "It was a less expensive way of sharing our photos [than] making hundreds of copies of photos and then mailing them out to everyone," Sara says.

Strangers also enjoy viewing the site. In fact, Sara says the Web site gets around five hundred hits per month. "We receive about ten e-mails a month from people asking questions about getting married in Greece. It's fun. It's the wedding that keeps on giving," she says.

CREATING A SCRAPBOOK

Another place to keep your wedding memories alive is a wedding scrapbook. Many courses are offered in scrapbooking, and the result is often a professional-looking keepsake that will last for generations.

WEDDING SOUVENIRS

Looking for a unique place to display your wedding photos? What about printing them on mugs, T-shirts, coasters, or aprons? CafePress.com (www.cafepress.com) enables you to have your photo emblazoned on a wide variety of products. Your wedding guests can purchase the products online.

ONLINE ALBUMS

Share your wedding photos online. Several sites offer free online photo albums. Check out www.ofoto.com, www.snapfish.com, or http://photos.yahoo.com.

One way to get started on your scrapbook is to have a scrapbooking party. Invite your family and friends over after the wedding, and have each person create a page of your wedding-day memories.

Darin and I didn't take any classes, but we made our own scrapbook. We bought a scrapbook album and some acid-free glue, then away we went. It took us only a few hours to put it all together. We included newspaper clippings, wedding lists, a menu, a wedding program, response cards, a napkin ring, an invitation, and many other wedding-related items. We also wrote notes to explain each item.

Twila and Daniel created a scrapbook that served as a guest book for their wedding. They placed inside the scrapbook forty different engagement photos by a professional photographer. During the reception, each guest chose a page on which to write a message for the couple. "Typically the guests left more of a greeting [rather] than just a signature," says Twila. After the wedding the couple added their wedding program, wedding flowers, and other wedding memorabilia to the scrapbook.

Susan also created a scrapbook instead of a traditional guest book. "I always found the traditional guest books somewhat impersonal. You wait in line and then sign your name and maybe give an address. There is just no warmth, joy, or happiness in that," Susan says.

Susan used a blank journal, calligraphy pens, photos, and photo mounting squares to make the scrapbook; it took about forty hours and cost about $60.

Before the wedding, Susan hunted down photographs of herself and Nikhil growing up. She also found photographs of friends and family members who would be attending the wedding. "I spent a week placing pictures, letters, and invitations in the journal. After the wedding, I added in pictures from the wedding festivities," she says.

On the couple's wedding day, friends and family wrote messages in the scrapbook. "We love our scrapbook. We look through it once a month to reread the warm wishes and look over the pictures," says Susan.

TIPS ON MAKING A SCRAPBOOK

- From the start of your wedding plans, save receipts, brochures, "to do" lists, magazine pages, printed Web pages, and any other items related to your wedding. Keep a scrapbook folder to store the items.

- Keep a journal of the planning process. Write down your feelings about your upcoming wedding. Include why you chose the ceremony and reception locations, why you chose your attendants, why you chose particular readings, etc.

- Having any showers or other prewedding parties? Take pictures to include in your scrapbook.

- Keep one each of your wedding invitations, wedding programs, and place cards; and keep a copy of your readings and marriage license. Place these in your scrapbook.

- Gather candid wedding photos to place in your scrapbook.

- Purchase a scrapbooking album that suits your style.

- Purchase acid-free scrapbooking paper and photo mounts or a glue stick.

- Invest in a good pair of scissors.

- If you want to add embellishments (stickers, tags, stamps, etc.) to your scrapbook, check out craft and scrapbooking stores in your area or online. You can also use clip art from your computer and simply print the images with a color printer.

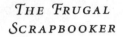

THE FRUGAL SCRAPBOOKER

If you're looking for good deals on scrapbooking supplies, check out eBay (www.ebay.com), where you will find an entire section on scrapbooking.

SHADOW BOXES AND STORAGE BOXES

Creating a shadow box with one or several of your favorite wedding mementos is a great way to preserve and display your wedding memories. You can place everything from a wedding invitation to your dried floral bouquet to a collage of wedding-day items inside a shadow box.

HOW TO MAKE A SHADOW BOX

- Purchase a shadow box. Make sure it is constructed out of acid-free material.

- Gather the items you want to display.

- Use fabric or acid-free paper to cover the backing—which should also be acid free. Choose paper or fabric that complements the memorabilia. Glue the fabric or paper to the backing using spray adhesive.

- Arrange the items on the backing.

- If you will insert dried or pressed flowers, spray them with a flower sealer first.

- Use white latex adhesive to attach your memorabilia to the backing.

- Put the frame together, then apply wrapping paper, wallpaper, or any other special paper (it doesn't have to be acid free) to the back of the shadow box. Write on the back a description of what is inside the box. You can even cover the back with a collage of wedding photos.

If you prefer, you can simply use a special storage box to hold your wedding memorabilia. Heather, whose hobby is bookbinding, made a unique storage box called a drop spine box (when the top of the box is opened, one of the sides drops open) for all of her wedding keepsakes. "We put in the guest book, all the returned [response] cards, [greeting] cards people gave us, the wedding programs, my veil, a copy of the readings our friends did in the ceremony . . . our vows, an invitation, a favor, and an invitation to my bridal shower," she says.

Hatboxes and gift boxes can act as storage boxes. You can also buy a simple box or container and decorate it yourself by painting it or using decoupage and dried flowers from your bouquet. If you use a cardboard box, make sure you keep it in a dry place so it doesn't mildew.

PRESERVING YOUR FLOWERS

To preserve your wedding flowers, you can press them, hang them to dry, or have them freeze-dried.

To press your flowers, place them in a book (use some absorbent paper between the pages to protect the book) or use a flower press. (Lee Valley Tools & Veritas Tools sells a microwave flower press that offers instant results. Check out www.leevalley.com.)

You can hang your flowers upside down in a dark, dry place. Drying time varies for different flowers; check them after a few days.

Christina and James did something unusual with their dried flowers. "We took the flowers from my bouquet and his boutonniere and dried them for use in a homemade candle," says Christina.

With the freeze-drying method, a machine removes water from the flowers while they are frozen. The process usually takes several weeks, and it works best on flowers that are fresh. The advantage of freeze-drying is that most flowers will retain their natural color and shape.

Jennifer chose to have her bouquet of purple lisianthus, sterling roses, and purple misty freeze-dried and placed in a glass dome, which she displays in her living room. "My bouquet doesn't look like it did on the wedding day, but it looks nice, and I love having it. It's a very special keepsake," she says.

KEEPING YOUR CAKE (AND EATING IT TOO!)

Darin and I had plenty of leftover scrumptious wedding cake. Instead of freezing a portion for our first anniversary, we—with help from our families—ate it the following day. No regrets here!

Some couples, in keeping with tradition and to bring good luck, preserve the top tier of their wedding cake to eat on their first anniversary.

TIPS FOR FREEZING YOUR WEDDING CAKE

- Ask a friend or relative to take care of the cake after the reception.

- Make sure the cake sits on foil or plastic beneath, not cardboard. Otherwise it will taste like cardboard.

- The cake should be placed in the freezer until the icing is hard (usually just a few minutes) then removed and wrapped with at least two layers of plastic wrap. A couple of layers of heavy-duty aluminum foil should follow.

- The cake should be placed inside a box and returned to the freezer, where it should stay until your first anniversary!

PRESERVING YOUR DRESS

When I found out how much it would cost to have my dress cleaned and boxed for storage, I gasped. Although I can be a real sentimentalist, preserving my dress wasn't that important to me—especially at such an expense! So instead of boxing it up, I took it to a resale shop, where, as I write this, it sits on a rack and waits for a buyer.

Other brides wouldn't dream of parting with their wedding dresses. Jennifer, for instance, felt it was essential to have her wedding gown professionally cleaned and boxed. "I knew from the beginning of this whole process that I would have my gown preserved for several reasons. First, I work at a museum and love history. I guess it's just in me to

KEEP IT
SEPARATED

If you pack your wedding gown in a box, wrap your headpiece separately. Otherwise the metal might deteriorate and ruin the fabric of your gown.

preserve and care for special things for the future. Also, I love my gown. I know every bride's gown is special to her, but mine is such an expression of my personality, I couldn't even think of getting rid of it. . . . I could never have sold it," she says.

TIPS ON PRESERVING YOUR WEDDING DRESS

- Have your dress professionally cleaned as soon after the wedding as you can, otherwise stains may become permanent. Make sure the professional cleaner you use is experienced in handling wedding gowns. Point out any stains that need attention.

- Remove shoulder pads and other items made of foam. They will deteriorate over time and could ruin the dress material.

- Once the dress is cleaned, store it properly. Do not simply hang your dress in a closet; this will stretch and weaken the fabric over time. Lay the gown flat, roll it, or fold it.

- If you decide to box the dress yourself, wear cotton gloves when handling your gown to prevent your skin from transferring oil onto the fabric.

- Using colorless acid-free tissue, fold and wrap your dress. Stuff the bodice and the sleeves (if there are any) with tissue so that the dress retains its shape. Also use tissue to pad creases.

- Place the dress in a lidded acid-free box, and store it under a bed or in a dry place at room temperature. Do not store your dress in an attic, basement, laundry room, or bathroom because of temperature and humidity levels. Make sure the place will not constantly expose the dress to ultraviolet or fluorescent light.

- Open the box each year so the dress can breathe. Refold it to prevent permanent creases.

OTHER WAYS TO KEEP THE MEMORIES ALIVE

Each couple seems to have a unique way of remembering their wedding. Darin and I enjoy viewing our wedding slides periodically; they take us right back to our special day. We also enjoy looking through our scrapbook. Here are some other ways couples keep their wedding memories alive:

An Anniversary Treat

If you're getting married at an inn or a bed-and-breakfast, part of your anniversary celebration each year can be to spend a night at the destination.

❧ "My husband has the 'family seal' I carved for him. It's made out of red cedar and tied to a silk cord. We used it to seal the wedding invitations by dipping it into melted wax. He wears the seal all of the time except when I'm traveling without him. Then he puts it around my neck as he kisses me good-bye. It acts as a pseudo good-luck charm and 'know I'm with you when we are apart' charm." —*Mellinda*

❧ "I feel that our wedding favors were picked with the idea of keeping the memory of our wedding alive. We gave each guest a Colorado blue spruce seedling in a silver bucket with planting instructions. Each envelope read, 'In honor of our life together.' Many of the guests, including my in-laws, have planted the seedlings. We will be buying a house in the next six months and will be transplanting one of the small trees to our own yard."—*Cari*

❧ "My husband's nephew taped our wedding using a digital video camera, and he later incorporated our photos (from childhood to dating to our wedding) and made it into a DVD."—*Christina*

RELIVING THE MOMENTS

Photographs, scrapbooks, journals, Web sites, and other memorabilia are all wonderful for reliving your wedding memories. Although some of these preservation methods can require a bit of time and effort, they're more than worth it. Your wedding day will go by fast, but if you take the time to capture and record it—with a scrapbook, a shadow box, a journal, or some other method—you will have keepsakes to make it last a lifetime. These keepsakes will spark your memories and inspire you to reminisce about that wonderful day in your life and share it over and over again with your loved ones.

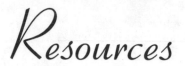

Resources

Here is a list of Web sites, organizations, and vendors that can assist you in creating your intimate wedding.

WEDDING PLANNING

Bliss! Weddings
www.blissweddings.com

Frugalbride.com
www.frugalbride.com

The Knot
www.theknot.com

Talk About Weddings
www.talkaboutweddings.com

Ultimatewedding.com
www.ultimatewedding.com

WeddingChannel.com
www.weddingchannel.com

Wedding Gazette
www.weddinggazette.com

BUDGET PLANNING

IhateFinancialPlanning.com
Tips for people who don't enjoy financial planning.
www.ihatefinancialplanning.com

WEDDING LICENSE

WeddingDetails.com
Information on license laws in various states.
www.weddingdetails.com/questions/license.cfm

WEDDING INSURANCE

WedSafe
Insurance that covers your wedding.
www.wedsafe.com
(877) 723-3933

Fireman's Fund
Offers wedding insurance.
www.firemansfund.com
(800) ENGAGED (364-2433)

Invitations

ORDERING INVITATIONS ONLINE

The American Stationery Company
www.theamericanwedding.com
(800) 428-0379

Message in a Bottle Shop
Send your invitation inside a bottle.
www.bottlemeamessage.com
(714) 441-3442

The Party Block
www.regencyinvitations.com
(800) 205-6400

Paper Style
www.paperstyle.com
(888) 670-5300

Wedding Invitations 411
www.weddinginvitations411.com
(877) 645-2793

CREATE YOUR OWN INVITATIONS

Lee Valley Tools Ltd.
Using pressed flowers on your invitations? Microwave flower presses can be purchased here.
www.leevalley.com
(800) 871-8158 (U.S.)
(800) 267-8767 (Canada)

Wedding Clipart
For clipart and templates for making your own invitations.
www.weddingclipart.com

Gift Registries

HONEYMOON REGISTRIES

HAVE GUESTS HELP PAY FOR YOUR HONEYMOON.

After I Do
www.afterido.com
(800) 956-4436

The Big Day
www.thebigday.com
(800) 304-1141

Giftpile.com
www.giftpile.com
(619) 227-4706

HoneyLuna.com
www.honeyluna.com
(800) 809-LUNA (5862)

STOCK REGISTRIES

REGISTER FOR STOCKS INSTEAD OF GIFTS.

Greenwish.com
www.greenwish.com
(888) 270-2757

CHARITABLE REGISTRIES

GUESTS CAN DONATE TO CHARITY INSTEAD OF BUYING GIFTS.

I Do Foundation
www.idofoundation.org
Justgive.org
www.justgive.org
(866) JUSTGIVE (587-8448)

Attire and Accessories

BUYING WEDDING ATTIRE ONLINE

Alfred Sung
www.alfredsungbridals.com
(989) 275-2100 (U.S.)
(416) 247-4628 (Canada)

Bridalheadpieces.com
www.bridalheadpieces.com
(888) 646-9654

The Bridal World
www.thebridalworld.com
(866) 594-9017

Cybergown
www.cybergown.com
(909) 444-1000

David's Bridal
www.davidsbridal.com
(888) 480-BRIDE

EBay
www.ebay.com

House of Brides
www.houseofbrides.com

Wedding Expressions
www.wedding expressions.com
(888) 659-5085

Wedding Trade
www.weddingtrade.com

WEDDING DRESS INFORMATION

Weddingplans.com
Provides information on the various styles and necklines of wedding dresses.
www.weddingplans.com.cy/accessories.htm

BRIDESMAID DRESS DONATION

The Glass Slipper Project
A Chicago-based charity that collects gently used dresses
for disadvantaged high school girls to wear to proms.
www.glassslipperproject.org
(312) 409-4139

Operation Fairy Dust
Similar to The Glass Slipper Project but operates out
of New York City.
www.altrue.net/site/nybacked/

Ceremony

DOVE RELEASE

White Dove Release Professionals
Learn the ins and outs of releasing birds at your
reception.
www.white-dove-releases.com/index.html

INTERFAITH CEREMONIES

Interfaith Marriage Referrals
Lists clergy that will marry interfaith couples.
www.interfaith.org/clergyfinder.asp

The Rabbinic Center for Research and Counseling
Offers a list (for a fee) of rabbis that will officiate at
interfaith ceremonies.
www.rcrconline.org
(908) 233-0419

ONLINE ORDINATION

The Universal Life Church
A nondenominational church that offers free ordination
to anyone that requests it.
www.ulc.org

Wedding Ministers Online
Offers certification via the Internet for a nominal fee.
www.uncas.net/wedding

WEDDING VOWS

HELP WITH PERSONALIZING YOUR WEDDING VOWS.

A Ceremony Designed for You
A variety of sample vows.
www.ultimatewedding.com/vows

Ultimatewedding.com
Includes a selection of sample vows.
www.ultimatewedding.com/articles/

Ultimatewedding.com
Words for the wine cup ceremony can be found at this
site.
www.weddingromance.com/poems/

WEDDING PROGRAM

Foreverwed.com
Looking for examples of wedding programs? Check out
this site.
www.foreverwed1.com/articles/programs/

WEATHER

United States Weather Pages
Want to know your wedding day weather? Check out
the United States Weather Pages planner.
www.uswx.com

Reception

PLACE CARDS

Cookies 'N Cream
What about edible place cards? This web site sells hand-
decorated cookie place cards.
www.cookiesncream.com
(888) 269-7643

Favorite Brand Name Recipes
Here's a recipe for cookie place card holders.
www.favoritebrandrecipes.com/Recipes/120/0918001
120.htm.
(888) 269-7643

Party Poofers
Place card holders in a variety of shapes, including stars, hearts, cherubs, and seashells.
www.partypoofers.com/holders.htm
(269) 503-0933

Placetile Designs
Order reusable handmade ceramic place cards at this Web site.
www.placetile.com
(404) 875-4426

Sweet Distinction
Impress your guests with chocolate place cards found at this Web site.
www.sweetdistinction.com
(888) 447-0611

WEDDING FAVORS

ONLINE SITES WITH A WIDE VARIETY OF FAVORS.

A Dream Wedding
Offers personalized cookie cutters in the shape of daisies, butterflies, or hearts. Also offers bottled bath salts.
www.adreamwedding.com
(561) 790-7719

Beaucoup
Heart-shaped sugar cubes in a glass tube, and personalized mint tins—among many other unique favors.
www.beau-coup.com/bestsellers.htm
(877) 988-BEAU (2328)

Best Wedding Favors
www.bestweddingfavors.com
(702) 580-3070

Coolpartystuff.com
What about a photo of the two of you not only made out of chocolate, but also framed in this decadent treat?
www.coolpartystuff.com
(888) 247-4219

Giftfavors.com
If you're having a beach wedding, and you feel like splurging on the favors, check out this Web site which sells leis made out of wrapped candy.
www.giftfavors.com/themes/coolanduniquethmed
favors.html
(732) 583-1943

Pro Magik Industries
This site offers candy bar wrappers that are personalized to include your names, wedding date, and even a photo.
www.photowrappers.com/weddings.html
(877) 754-1478

Splendidpalate.com
For something edible and elegantly wrapped, there's French honey wrapped in white organza, as well as a variety of other unique favors.
www.splendidpalate.com/eventfavors.html
(877) 773-6637

Wedding-Favors-Etc.com
www.wedding-favors-etc.com

GUEST BOOKS

Guestbook Store
This site offers a neat concept for couples that want more than just autographs from their wedding guests.
www.guestbookstore.com

WEDDING DECORATIONS

Special Day Flowers
Silk and paper flowers.
www.weddingsandflowers.com
(877) 429-7257

BALLOONS

Balloons Galore
Balloons for your wedding reception.
www.balloons-galore.net
(906) 753-2665

LIQUOR

CAN'T FIGURE OUT HOW MUCH TO SERVE?
CHECK OUT THIS WEB SITE.

Moneycops.com
Another more-detailed wedding and catering calculator.
www.moneycops.com

CHOCOLATE FOUNTAINS
AND SCULPTURES

The Chocolate Fountain.com
Wow your guests with a chocolate fountain, for dipping fruit and other foods.
www.thechocolatefountain.com
(316) 636-4443

Eaton's Stores
You've heard of ice sculptures at weddings, but what about chocolate sculptures?
www.nhwedding.com/eatonschocolates/candy.html
(603) 623-1433

DESSERTS AND WEDDING CAKE

Cupcaketree.com
Looking for an alternative to a wedding cake? What about a cupcake tree?
www.cupcaketree.com
(866) 422-8733

FOOD DONATION

America's Second Harvest
America's Second Harvest will pick up leftover food and distribute it to people in need.
www.secondharvest.org
(800) 771-2303

Photography

FreeWeddingCameras.com
A variety of disposable cameras.
www.freeweddingcameras.com
(888) 688-0778

Professional Photographers of America
Lists photographers who are members of the Professional Photographers of America.
www.ppa.com
(800) 786-6277

Wedding Locations

BED-AND-BREAKFASTS AND INNS

BedandBreakfast.com
More than 27,000 bed-and-breakfasts throughout the world are listed here.
www.bedandbreakfast.com

Bed and Breakfast Inns Online
This Web site has details on more than 4,500 bed-and-breakfasts—and it has plenty of pictures to boot!
www.bbonline.com
(615) 868-1946

CharmingCountryInns.com
This Web site lists hundreds of little known, out-of-the-way inns and bed-and-breakfasts throughout North America.
www.charmingcountryinns.com

Emerson Inn by the Sea
1 Cathedral Avenue
Rockport, MA 01966
www.emersoninnbythesea.com
(800) 964-5550

Inn. St. Gemme Beauvais
78 North Main Street
Sainte Genevieve, MO 63670
www.bbhost.com/innstgemme
(800) 818-5744

MUSEUMS/HISTORIC SITES AND BUILDINGS

A Place in Time
Toni Boyles
P.O. Box 87
Tecumseh, KA 66542
www.aplaceintimeonline.com
(785) 379-8463

Chief Hosa Lodge
27661 Genesee Drive
Golden, CO 80401
www.chiefhosa.com
(888) CHIEF HOSA (244-3346)

Edgar Allan Poe Museum
1914-16 East Main Street
Richmond, VA 23223
www.poemuseum.org/about_the_museum/
(888) 21E-APOE (213-2763)

Wrigley Mansion Club
2501 East Telawa Trail
Phoenix, AZ 85016
www.wrigleymansionclub.com
(602) 553-7383

ART GALLERIES

The Andy Warhol Museum
117 Sandusky Street
Pittsburgh, PA 15212
www.warhol.org
(412) 237-8300

Fuller Museum of Arts
455 Oak Street
Brockton, MA 02301
www.fullermuseum.org
(508) 588-6000

LODGES

See Chief Hosa Lodge under
"Museums/Historic Sites and Buildings."

VINEYARDS

Castoro Cellars
P.O. Box 954
Templeton, CA 93465
www.castorocellars.com
(888) DAM-FINE (326-3463)

UNIQUE VENUES

Adventure Rabbi, Inc.
www.adventurerabbi.com
(303) 443-2642

Annointed Weddings of Maui
P.O. Box 11743
Lahaina Maui, HI 96761
www.maui.net/~anointed
(800) 962-7622

Aurora Ice Hotel
www.chenahotsprings.com/icehotel.html
(800) 478-4681

CC Africa Safaris and Tours
www.afroventures.com
(888) 88-AFRICA

Central Park Conservatory Garden
105th Street at 5th Avenue
www.centralpark.org
(212) 360-2766

Christa McAuliffe Planetarium
2 Institute Drive
Concord, NH 03301
www.starhop.com
(603) 271-STAR (271-7827)

Ice Hotel Quebec-Canada
143, route Duchesnay
Pavillon l'Aigle
Saint-Catherine-de-la-Jacques-Cartier
Québec, Canada G0A 3M0
www.icehotel-canada.com
(877) 505-0423

Jule's Undersea Lodge
51 Shoreland Drive
Key Largo, FL 33037
www.jul.com
(305) 451-2353

Mackinac Island
www.mackinac.com

Mall of America/Chapel of Love
345 East Broadway
Bloomington, MN 55425
www.chapeloflove.com
(800) 299-LOVE (299-5683)

Maverick Helicopter Tours
6075 Las Vegas Boulevard South
Las Vegas, NV 89119
www.maverickhelicopter.com
(888) 261-4414

Mojo Luxury Yacht
www.luxuryyachtweddings.com
(949) 574-4355

Orange Blossom Balloons
www.orangeblossomballoons.com
(407) 239-7677

Pearson's Pond Luxury Inn and Spa
4541 Sawa Circle
Juneau, AK 99801
www.pearsonspond.com
(888) 658-6328

Pioneertown
www.pioneertown.com

Santa Fe Southern Railway
410 South Guadalupe Street
Sante Fe, NM 87501
www.sfsr.com
(888) 989-8600

Seaworld Orlando
7007 Seaworld Drive
Orlando, FL 32821
www.buschgardens.com/seaworld/fla/prog_en.aspx
(407) 363-2273
(800) 327-2424 (press 3, then 1)

Spiritual Weddings
P.O. Box 877
Sante Fe, NM 87504
www.spiritualweddings.com
(505) 982-3779

Theme Weddings

Ask Ginka Wedding and Party Guide
Looking for ideas? This Web site has 500 theme ideas.
www.askginka.com/themes

Todays-Weddings.com
Suggestions on how to bring a theme into your wedding.
www.todays-weddings.com/planning/themes.php

Weddingthemes.com
Offers detailed information on everything from medieval weddings to beach weddings.
www.weddingthemes.com

MEDIEVAL AND RENAISSANCE

Medieval and Renaissance Wedding Page
Useful information on medieval weddings.
www.drizzle.com/~celyn/mrwp/mrwp.html

Medieval and Renaissance Wedding Ring
Having a medieval wedding? Join the medieval and Renaissance Wedding Ring at this Web site.
www.midnightgarden.com/wedding/mrwring.html

The Medieval and Renaissance Wedding Site
This Web site has plenty of links on medieval weddings.
www.midnightgarden.com/wedding/

Medieval Historical Societies
A list of medieval historical societies and organizations.
www.deremilitari.org

VICTORIAN

The Victorian Era: Part One—Preparation
A site devoted to the Victorian era.
www.literary-liaisons.com/article003.html

The Victorian Wedding
Provides historical information on the era.
www.lahacal.org/wed.html

THE ROARING TWENTIES

Reason to Party
This site offers a variety of ideas on hosting a roaring twenties party. Many of the suggestions can be applied to a wedding.
www.reasontoparty.com/roaringtwenties.htm

The Roaring Twenties and the Great Depression
If you are looking for information on the roaring twenties, check out this Web site.
http://users.snowcrest.net/jmike/

IRISH

Irish Wedding Customs and Traditions
Provides information on traditional Irish customs.
www.hudsonvalleyweddings.com/guide/irish.htm

Wedding Gazette
Offers ten ways to have an Irish Wedding.
www.weddinggazette.com

JAPANESE

JapaneseWeddingFavors.com
A great selection of Japanese wedding favors.
www.japaneseweddingfavors.com
(952) 758-1921

Things Japanese
Offers information on the history of Japanese weddings, as well as customs and rituals.
http://mothra.rerf.or.jp/ENG/Hiroshima/Things/81.html

MEXICAN

Hotlix
Tequila-flavored lollipops—complete with worm can be found at this site.
www.hotlix.com/wormpops.htm
(800) EAT-WORM (328-9676)

Jelly Belly
Want a unique favor for your Mexican-themed wedding? Try margarita, jalapeno, and lemon-lime jellybeans.
www.jellybelly.com
(888) 862-8952

La Tortilla Loca
Microwave tortilla warmers make unique favors.
www.latortillaloca.com
(520) 761-1544

NEW ORLEANS

MardiGrasStore.com
Check out a King Cake, a popular New Orleans cake.
www.mardigrasstore.com/catalog/king_cakes/index.html
(800) 259-8954

WESTERN

Western Colorado Wedding Guide
Looking for ideas for a Western-themed wedding?
Check this out.
www.westerncoweddings.com

Partymerchant.com
This site has lots of ideas for Western-themed nuptials.
www.partymerchant.com

Destination Weddings

PLANNING

DestinationBride.com
A helpful resource that provides information on desti-
nation weddings around the world.
www.destinationbride.com

The Destination and Specialty Wedding Page
Help in planning a unique wedding. Includes destina-
tion weddings.
www-personal.umich.edu/~kzaruba/wedding.html

WeddingsAbroad.com
A site that offers wedding-planning services throughout
the world. Includes articles, a discussion forum, feature
weddings, information on legal requirements, as well as
a destination directory.
www.weddingsabroad.com

Wholly Matrimony!
This site has a wide variety of information on destina-
tion weddings, including couple profiles, a discussion
forum, articles on planning, a FAQ on destination
weddings, as well as links to other Web sites.
www.whollymatrimony.com

CURRENCY CONVERTER

Xe.com
Want to find out how your currency fares in other
countries?
www.xe.com

CRUISE SHIP WEDDINGS

Carnival.com
www.carnival.com
(800) 933-4968

HollandAmerica.com
www.hollandamerica.com/onboard/weddings.do
(888) 475-5511

RoyalCaribbean.com
www.royalcaribbean.com/allaboutcruising/
weddings/packages/home.do
(888) 933-7225

BAHAMAS

The Bahamian
www.coordinators.thebahamian.com

Bahama Travel Net
www.bahamatravelnet.com/tips/wedfaq.html
(800) 330-8272

Geographia
Requirements for obtaining a marriage license in the
Bahamas.
www.geographia.com/bahamas/bsmarr02.htm
(242) 322-3316

ST. LUCIA

Geographia
www.geographia.com/st-lucia/lcmarr01.htm

St. Lucia Hotel and Tourism Association
Requirements for weddings in St. Lucia.
P.O. Box 545 Castries
St. Lucia, West Indies
www.stluciatravel.com.lc/weddings.htm
(758) 452-5978

BERMUDA

Bermuda Vacation Travel Guide
www.bermudatravelnet.com
(800) 330-8272

WeddingChannel.com
http://wedding.weddingchannel.com/travel/frommers/Bermuda/overview/index.asp

Wedding-Club.com
www.seattle.wedding-club.com/travel/bermuda.html

BRITISH COLUMBIA, CANADA

Government of British Columbia
Requirements for getting married in British Columbia.
www.vs.gov.bc.ca/marriage/howto.html

Virtual Cities
www.virtualcities.com/ons/bc/bcwedding.htm

Worldweb.com
Weddings in the Canadian Rockies.
www.bcrockies.worldweb.com/FeaturesReviews/PlanningaWedding/

FLORIDA

Disney Fairytale Weddings and Honeymoons
www.disney.go.com/vacations/disneyweddings
(321) 939-4610

Top Wedding Links
www.topweddinglinks.com

GREECE

Matt's Greece Travel Guide
Marriage requirements for Greece.
www.greecetravel.com/weddings/

Greece Travel Online
www.greecetravelonline.com

Hotel Esperas
Oia, 84702
Santorini Island
Cyclades, Greece
www.esperas-santorini.com
(+30) 22860-71088

Magicaljourneys.com
www.magicaljourneys.com/Travel/

HAWAII

Hawaii Bride and Groom Magazine
www.hawaiibride.com

PreviewHawaii.com
www.previewhawaii.com

ITALY

Getting Married in Italy
www.initaly.com/weddings/getmarried.htm

Italy Weddings
www.italyweddings.com

WeddingItaly.com
Paperwork requirements for Italy.
www.weddingitaly.com

JAMAICA

Getawayweddings.com
www.getawayweddings.com/articles/article-details.asp?ID=122

Lovetripper.com
www.lovetripper.com/channels/caribbean-weddings.html

Visitjamaica.com
www.visitjamaica.com/vacation_themes/weddings_and_honeymoons/default.aspx

LAKE TAHOE

TahoeWeddings.com
www.tahoeweddings.com

TahoeWeddings.org
www.tahoeweddings.org

LAS VEGAS

Getawayweddings.com
www.getawayweddings.com/las-vegas-weddings.html

LasVegasWeddings.com
www.las-vegas-wedding.net

Little Chapel of the Flowers
1717 Las Vegas Boulevard South
Las Vegas, NV 89104
www.littlechapel.com
(800) 843-2410

Stratosphere Casino Hotel and Tower
www.stratospherehotel.com
(800) 998-6937 general
(888) 236-7495 reservations

Vegas.com
Requirements for a marriage license in Nevada.
www.vegas.com/weddings/legal.html

Viva Las Vegas Wedding Chapel
1205 Las Vegas Boulevard South
Las Vegas, NV 89104
www.vivalasvegasweddings.com
(800) 574-4450

MEXICO

Lovetripper.com
www.lovetripper.com/channels/wedding-mexico.html

MexOnline.com
www.mexonline.com/wedding.htm

SCOTLAND

Culzean Castle
Maybole
Ayrshire, KA19 8LE
Scotland, UK
www.culzeancastle.net/functions.html
(011-44) 1655 884455

Romantic Scotland
www.visitscotland.com/aboutscotland/

Scottish Wedding Consultants
Chamber House
42/3 Hardengreen Business Park
Dalhousie Road
Dalkeith
Midlothian
EH22 3NU
Scotland, UK
www.scottishweddingconsultants.co.uk
(011-44) 131-561-6281

Scottish Weddings Online
www.scottishweddingsonline.co.uk

VIRGIN ISLANDS

USVI
www.usviguide.com/stjohn/stjwed.htm

The Virgin Islands Best Online Guide
www.vinow.com

The Westin St. John Resort and Villas
USVI
P.O. Box 8310
Great Cruz Bay
St. John, U.S. Virgin Islands
00831
www.westinresortstjohn.com
(340) 693-8000 ext. 1908
(888) 627-7206 general

Tying the Knot...Again

Bride Again
Bride Again is an online magazine that discusses a variety of issues regarding second weddings.
www.brideagain.com

GettingRemarried.com
An informative site that discusses everything from wording invitations to financial planning. Also discusses legality issues of second marriages, and has a message board.
www.gettingremarried.com

Hudson Valley Weddings
Looking for etiquette info on second weddings? This Web site will provide you with plenty of information on the rules of saying "I do" again.
www.hudsonvalleyweddings.com/guide/2nd-wed.htm

Creating Wedding Memories

ONLINE PHOTO ALBUMS

Place your wedding photos online at these Web sites.

Ofoto
www.ofoto.com

Snapfish
www.snapfish.com

Yahoo! Photos
http://photos.yahoo.com

PRODUCTS WITH YOUR WEDDING PHOTOS

Cafepress.com
This Web site enables you to have the wedding photo of your choice
emblazoned on a wide variety of products including mugs, coasters, aprons, T-shirts, and hats.
www.cafepress.com

PHOTO MONTAGE

PhotoInnovation.com
This site gives some examples of photomontage.
www.photoinnovation.com

Photography Credits

author photo: Ng's Photography, Ontario, Canada; (519) 735-7659

page 17: Leon Wild, Reades Wild Studio, Ontario, Canada; (519) 981-5562

page 42: Armand LeConte

page 65: Lee Krohn, Lee Krohn Photography, LLC, Manchester Center, Vermont; (802) 362-7049;
e-mail: pianopix@sover.net

page 86: Frank Frost, Frank Frost Photography, Albuquerque, New Mexico; (505) 293-2724;
www.FrankFrost.com; e-mail: Frank@FrankFrost.com

page 105: Taina Cruzado Cote, Boston, Massachusetts; (888) 288-0434 or (617) 254-8989;
www.tainacruzado.com

page 121: Matt Peyton, Matt Peyton Photography, New York, New York; (212) 452-3267; www.peyton.com;
e-mail: matt@peyton.com

page 142: Gene Keenum, Murphy, North Carolina; (828) 644-5294; e-mail: genekeenum333@hotmail.com

page 159: Clive Wright, Island Photos, Santorini, Greece; e-mail: clivepix@otenet.gr

page 172: D W Pena, Rocklin, California; e-mail: dpena@surewest.net

Bibliography

BOOKS

Roney, Carley. *The Knot's Complete Guide to Weddings in the Real World*. New York: Broadway Books, 1998.

WEB SITES AND ONLINE ARTICLES

Alicia Abell, and Robyn Gearey. "Isn't it Romantic." *Washingtonian* Online—Wedding Guide. www.washington ian.com/weddings/isntitromantic.html, posted January 2002

Barker, Olivia. "Couples Do Variations on Marriage Themes." USATODAY.com. www.usatoday.com/life/2001-06-26-theme-weddings.htm, posted June 26, 2001.

"Bridal Industry Statistics." The Knot. www.theknot.com/au_industrystats.shtml, downloaded March 10, 2003

Ebenkamp, Becky. "We've Only Just Begun . . . To Freak Out!" *Brandweek*. www.findarticles.com/cf_dls/m0BDW/19_42/74521281/p1/article.jhtml, posted May 7, 2001.

Libaw, Oliver. "'I Do' Differently." ABCNews.com. http://abcnews.go.com/sections/us/DailyNews/elopement020423.html, posted April 23, 2002.

Paul, Pamela. "Going Off to Get Married." *Time* Online Edition. www.time.com/time/connections/printout/0,8816,1101030512-450264,00.html, posted May 7, 2003.

Takahama, Valerie. "Lavish Ceremonies Aren't Just for First-Time Brides and Grooms." *The Orange County Register* www.azcentral.com/weddings/articles/secondbride.html, downloaded January 15, 2004.

"Wedding Facts and Trends." Hallmark Press Room. http://pressroom.hallmark.com/wedding_facts.html, download January 15, 2004.

"Weddings: Millie Martini Bratten" USATODAY.com. www.usatoday.com/community/chat/0606brides.htm, posted June 6, 2002.

Wilson, Craig. "Going to a Castle and They're Gonna Get Married." USATODAY.com. www.usatoday.com/life/travel/leisure/2001/2001-03-09-castles.htm, posted October 29, 2001.

INDEX

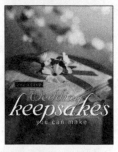